Certificate in Business Accounting

BA4: Fundamentals of Ethics, Corporate Governance and Business Law

For exams from January 2024

Exam Practice Kit

In this edition

- Banks of objective test questions across the whole syllabus
- Answers with detailed feedback
- Advice on exam technique

Seventh edition 2023

ISBN 9781 0355 0788 7
Previous ISBN 9781 0355 0275 2
eISBN 9781 0355 0824 2

British Library Cataloguing-in-Publication Data
A catalogue record for this book is available from the British Library

Published by

BPP Learning Media Ltd
BPP House, Aldine Place
142-144 Uxbridge Road
London W12 8AA

learningmedia.bpp.com

Printed in the United Kingdom

Your learning materials, published by BPP Learning Media Ltd, are printed on paper obtained from traceable sustainable sources.

We are grateful to the Chartered Institute of Management Accountants for permission to reproduce past examination questions. The suggested solutions in the exam answer bank have been prepared by BPP Learning Media Ltd.

AICPA & CIMA
Registered Tuition Provider

BPP
LEARNING
MEDIA

Contents

Question and Answer index

Using your BPP Exam Practice Kit

One of the key criteria for achieving exam success is question practice. There is generally a direct correlation between candidates who study all topics and practise exam questions and those who are successful in their exams. This Kit gives you ample opportunity for such practice throughout your preparations for your OT exam.

All questions in your exam are compulsory and all the component learning outcomes will be examined so you must **study the whole syllabus**. Selective studying will limit the number of questions you can answer and hence reduce your chances of passing.

Practising as many exam-style questions as possible will be the key to passing this exam. You must do questions under **timed conditions** as part of your preparations.

Breadth of question coverage

Questions will cover the whole of the syllabus so you must study all the topics in the syllabus.

The weightings in the table below indicate the approximate proportion of study time you should spend on each topic, and is related to the number of questions per syllabus area in the exam.

BA4: Fundamentals of Ethics, Corporate Governance & Business Law Syllabus topics	Weighting
A Business Ethics and Ethical Conflict	30%
B Corporate Governance, Controls and Corporate Social Responsibility	45%
C General Principles of Legal System, Contract and Employment Law	15%
D Company Administration	10%

Errata

BPP Learning Media do everything possible to ensure the material is accurate and up to date when sending to print. In the event that any errors are found after the print date, they are uploaded to the following website: https://learningmedia.bpp.com/catalog?pagename=Errata

The Exam

The exam is a computer based assessment, which is available on demand at assessment centres all year round.

The exams at Certificate Level can be taken in any order, but candidates must pass or be exempt from them all before they can move on to the Operational Level.

Each exam lasts for two hours and will contain 85 questions.

The exam will be made up of different types of questions, as shown below:

Question Type	Explanation
Multiple choice	Standard multiple choice items provide four options. One option is correct and the other three are incorrect. Incorrect options will be plausible, so you should expect to have to use detailed, syllabus-specific knowledge to identify the correct answer rather than relying on common sense.
Multiple response	A multiple response item is the same as a multiple choice question, except more than one response is required. You will be told how many options you need to select.
Number entry	Number entry (or 'fill in the blank') questions require you to type a short numerical response. You should carefully follow the instructions in the question in terms of how to type your answer – eg the correct number of decimal places
Drag and drop	Drag and drop questions require you to drag a 'token' onto a pre-defined area. These tokens can be images or text. This type of question is effective at testing the order of events, labelling a diagram or linking events to outcomes.
Hot spot	These questions require you to identify an area or location on an image by clicking on it. This is commonly used to identify a specific point on a graph or diagram.
Item set	Two–four questions all relating to the same short scenario. Each question will be 'standalone', such that your ability to answer subsequent questions in the set does not rely on getting the first one correct.

Passing the Exam

- Read, and **re-read the question** to ensure you fully understand what is being asked.

- When starting to read a question, especially one with a lengthy scenario, **read the requirement first**. You will then find yourself considering the requirement as you read the data in the scenario, helping you to focus on exactly what you have to do.

- **Do not spend too much time on one question** – remember you should spend slightly less than 1.5 minutes, on average, per question.

- If you cannot decide between two answers – look carefully and decide whether for one of the options you are making an unnecessary assumption – **do not be afraid of trusting your gut instinct.**

- **Do not keep changing your mind** – research has shown that the first answer that appeals to you is often the correct one.

- Remember that marks are awarded for correct answers, and marks will not be deducted for incorrect answers. Therefore **answer every single question**, even ones you are unsure of.

- Always submit an answer for a given question even if you do not know the answer – **never leave any answers blank.**

- **Pace yourself** – you will need to work through the exam at the right speed. Too fast and your accuracy may suffer, too slow and you may run out of time. Use this Kit to practise your time keeping and approach to answering each question.

- If you are unsure about anything, remember to **ask the test administrator** before the test begins.

- Remember to **keep moving on!** You may be presented with a question which you simply cannot answer due to difficulty or if the wording is too vague. If you find yourself spending five minutes determining the answer for a question then your time management skills are poor and you are wasting valuable time.

- If you finish the exam with time to spare, use the rest of the time to **review your answers** and to make sure that you answered every question.

Questions

1 The importance of ethics

1   Public sector employees, including accountants, are governed by 'The Seven Principles of Public Life'.

   Which of the following principles requires conflicts of interest to be declared?

   ○   Leadership
   ○   Honesty
   ○   Accountability
   ○   Integrity

2   Ethical codes such as those developed by IFAC and CIMA should:

   ○   Enhance the standards of behaviour of members
   ○   Eliminate unethical behaviour by members
   ○   Indicate the highest level of behaviour expected of members
   ○   Always consist of fundamental principles

3   How does a framework-based approach to developing an ethical code differ from a rules-based approach?

   ○   It sets out specific guidance for each specific ethical dilemma.
   ○   It expects members to adhere to the letter of the law.
   ○   It expects members to embody certain principles.
   ○   The governing body anticipates all potential ethical problems.

4   Which of the following is a characteristic of the framework-based approach to a code of ethics?

   ○   Explicit
   ○   Judgement
   ○   Detection
   ○   Rules

5   Which of the following are the names given to the role within an organisation that has responsibilities for overseeing the application of its ethical policies and as a point of contact to help employees resolve ethical dilemmas?

   Select all that apply.

   ☐   Policy officer
   ☐   Compliance officer
   ☐   Integrity officer
   ☐   Ethical officer

6   Which THREE of the following bodies make up the FRC's Codes and Standards Committee?

☐   Audit and Assurance Council
☐   Corporate Reporting Council
☐   Corporate Reporting Review Committee
☐   Case Management Committee
☐   Actuarial Council

7   What are ethics?

○   Personal principles that guide behaviour
○   Religious rules that determine an individual's actions
○   Principles that guide how individuals should work together for a common goal
○   Professional guidance that guides behaviour

8   How does a rules-based approach to developing an ethical code differ from a framework-based approach?

○   It sets out fundamental principles for members to follow.
○   It attempts to anticipate every possible ethical dilemma.
○   It offers general guidelines for specific circumstances.
○   Members are expected to comply with the spirit of the code rather than the letter of the law.

9   Which of the following statements concerning codes of ethics is incorrect?

○   IFAC's code is based on compliance principles.

○   The code of ethics of a business may take either a rules-based or framework-based approach.

○   CIMA's code is based on an ethical framework.

○   Many codes of ethics require individuals to respect the spirit of the law rather than the letter of the law.

10   Why has IFAC issued a global code of ethics for accountants?

○   It was requested to do so by the World Bank.
○   Worldwide corporate scandals have eroded all confidence in accountants.
○   To enhance the quality and standards of services provided by accountants.
○   International law has required a worldwide code of ethics.

11   Alun is employed in his organisation's finance team. When making ethical decisions, Alun looks to maximise his own personal outcomes and to look after his own needs. Alun's personal approach to ethics is:

○   Pluralist
○   Absolutist
○   Relativist
○   Egotist

12 Which TWO of the following are members of the FRC?

☐ CSC
☐ CIMA
☐ CC
☐ IFAC

13 Which of the following is a role of the Conduct Committee?

○ Commenting on proposed changes to international standards
○ Advising on draft codes and standards
○ Audit quality reviews
○ Issuing ethical standards

14 Which of the following is a role of the Codes and Standards Committee?

○ Advising on draft codes and standards
○ Audit quality reviews
○ Professional discipline
○ Oversight of the regulation of accountants

15 Which THREE of the following are characteristics of the framework approach to ethical codes?

☐ Discretionary
☐ Implicit
☐ Prevention
☐ Detection
☐ Mandatory

2 CIMA's code of ethics

1 CIMA's code of ethics has several purposes. Which of the following is one of those purposes?

○ It provides members with all of their legal obligations in one document.
○ It is evidence that all CIMA members meet IFAC's requirements for ethical behaviour.
○ It is a requirement of its status as a chartered organisation.
○ It can be used to judge the behaviour of members under CIMA's disciplinary procedures.

2 Which of the following statements best describes the relationship between the Code of Ethics of CIMA and the Code of Ethics of IFAC?

○ CIMA's framework is generally the same as IFAC's with some amendments to ensure it meets other regulatory requirements.

○ IFAC provides the detailed rules that CIMA must include in its code.

○ CIMA has picked the most important elements of the IFAC code for inclusion into its own.

○ IFAC's code is based on international standards whereas CIMA's is specific to the UK.

3 According to the CGMA report on responsible business, the application of ethical principles to business behaviour is:

- O   Ethical performance
- O   Responsible business
- O   Ethical management information
- O   Business ethics

4 Under which circumstance may an accountant have to disclose information given to them in confidence?

- O   When requested by a regulator
- O   When requested by a lawyer
- O   When requested by a fellow employee or client
- O   When requested by an employer

5 A colleague has provided a report to senior management knowing that it that contains misleading information.

Which of CIMA's fundamental principles have they broken?

- O   Integrity
- O   Confidentiality
- O   Professional competence and due care
- O   Objectivity

6 An accountant develops constructive relationships with their colleagues, and values the rights and opinions that they have.

Which personal virtue do they display?

- O   Responsibility
- O   Timeliness
- O   Respect
- O   Courtesy

7 An accountant recognises that when their judgements and decisions are called into question, they are ultimately responsible. Which of the following professional qualities are they demonstrating?

- O   Independence
- O   Accountability
- O   Social responsibility
- O   Scepticism

8 An accountant who refuses to take on work as they do NOT have any experience in that area can be said to be arguing what?

- O   Integrity
- O   Professional behaviour
- O   Objectivity
- O   Professional competence

9   Which type of threat to an accountant's fundamental principles is described below?

The threat that a professional accountant will promote a client's or employer's position to the extent that their objectivity is compromised.

- ○   Familiarity threat
- ○   Self-interest threat
- ○   Intimidation threat
- ○   Advocacy threat

---

10   Which of the following situations may create a conflict of interest?

Select all that apply.

- ☐   Working part-time for two rival businesses
- ☐   Owning shares in a company that competes with your employer
- ☐   Being employed by a close relative
- ☐   Being offered a valuable gift by a friend who is also a business contact
- ☐   Receiving a performance bonus from your manager

---

11   Which THREE of the following allow accountants to demonstrate the professional quality of scepticism?

- ☐   By keeping their mind free from distractions
- ☐   By seeking supporting evidence before accepting information is accurate
- ☐   By investigating why information was given to them
- ☐   By reviewing the work of a junior before accepting it as correct
- ☐   By being straightforward and honest at all times

---

12   It has been brought to your attention that a colleague in your accounts department has been continually submitting inflated expenses claims.

Which of CIMA's fundamental principles have they breached?

- ○   Objectivity
- ○   Professional competence
- ○   Professional behaviour
- ○   Confidentiality

---

13   Which of CIMA's fundamental principles is described below?

Accountants should act fairly and not allow prejudice, bias, or the influence of others to affect their judgements.

- ○   Integrity
- ○   Confidentiality
- ○   Professional competence and due care
- ○   Objectivity

---

14   Which type of threat to an accountant's fundamental principles is also known as a conflict of interest?

    ○   Advocacy threat
    ○   Familiarity threat
    ○   Self-interest threat
    ○   Self-review threat

15   Why is it important for a CIMA member to follow the concept of lifelong learning?

    ○   To develop their assertiveness skills
    ○   As the accounting environment is constantly evolving
    ○   As they are legally required to do so
    ○   To make sure they are more skilled than accountants from other accountancy bodies

3 Ethical dilemmas

1   An accountant has decided to change an accounting policy, contrary to established accounting standards, on the request of their manager, because the existing policy does not fit with business strategy. Which sets of values are conflicting?

    ○   Corporate and personal
    ○   Professional and personal
    ○   Professional and corporate
    ○   Professional and societal

2   Which of the following examples of unethical behaviour could result in an accountant facing criminal prosecution?

    ○   Sending a rude email to a colleague
    ○   Supplying confidential information about the company's financial results in exchange for gifts
    ○   Supplying management accounts to directors that are inaccurate
    ○   Allowing personal problems to interfere with the production of management accounts

3   Which of the following are potential consequences to the accounting profession if members are allowed to behave unethically?

    Select all that apply.

    ☐   Professional bodies may lose their 'chartered' status
    ☐   Increased regulation of the profession by external organisations
    ☐   Increased employability of accountants
    ☐   Improved reputation of the profession
    ☐   Reduced public trust in the profession

4   What should a CIMA member do if the only option available to resolve an ethical issue with their employer involves breach of confidentiality?

    ○   Proceed with the solution
    ○   Take legal advice before proceeding
    ○   Do not proceed with the resolution
    ○   Take advice from friends and family

5   Which of the following are CIMA students and members primarily obliged to follow above all the other options?

    ○   The law
    ○   CIMA's Ethical Code
    ○   The terms of their employment contract
    ○   The terms of any relevant business contracts

6   Which of CIMA's fundamental principles has been breached below?

A shareholder contacts the company's Finance Director complaining about the results contained in the management accounts. The Finance Director replies giving operational reasons for the poor results.

    ○   Objectivity
    ○   Integrity
    ○   Professional competence
    ○   Confidentiality

7   Which of the following is categorised as a financial stakeholder in a company?

    ○   The media
    ○   Activist groups
    ○   Competitors
    ○   The Government

8   Which THREE of the following should CIMA members do while attempting to resolve an ethical issue?

    ☐   Check all the facts
    ☐   Decide if the issue is legal in nature
    ☐   Identify affected parties
    ☐   Document their day to day feelings
    ☐   Seek advice from their families

9   Which of the following is NOT a consideration that an accountant should have when resolving an ethical issue?

    ○   Transparency
    ○   Effect
    ○   Fairness
    ○   Cost

10   Your manager has set out a new policy that you should follow when preparing the management accounts. From now on you are to use estimates for trade receivables and payables. Does this conflict with any of CIMA's fundamental principles, and if so which one?

- ○   No, it does not conflict with any of CIMA's principles
- ○   Integrity
- ○   Objectivity
- ○   Professional competence and due care

11   When a CIMA member faces an ethical conflict, who should they look to first to resolve it?

- ○   CIMA
- ○   The Board of Directors
- ○   Themselves
- ○   Relevant outside professional advisers

12   In the event of an accountant's professional ethics being in conflict with a contractual obligation, what course of action should be taken?

- ○   The accountant should meet their contractual obligation at the expense of their professional ethics.
- ○   The accountant should follow their professional ethics at the expense of their contractual obligation.
- ○   The accountant should act in accordance with their personal ethics.
- ○   The accountant should follow any advice given to them by their employer.

13   You are working as an assistant management accountant in a large manufacturing company and your role involves costing new products. A long-time supplier has invited you and your colleagues out for lunch.

Do you have an ethical dilemma?

- ○   No dilemma
- ○   Yes, a risk of breaking integrity
- ○   Yes, a risk of breaking objectivity
- ○   Yes, a risk of breaking confidentiality

14   Your manager has passed you their work for you to double-check. You find a large number of errors but your manager insists it is fine and tells you to send it to the Finance Director.

Do you have an ethical dilemma?

- ○   No dilemma
- ○   Yes, a risk of breaking objectivity
- ○   Yes, a risk of breaking integrity
- ○   Yes, a risk of breaking confidentiality

15   Where a professional duty conflicts with the law, which should be followed?

- ○   The professional duty
- ○   The professional duty if it agrees with the individual's personal ethics
- ○   The law
- ○   The law, only it if agrees with the individual's personal ethics

4 The meaning of corporate governance

1   Corporate governance rules are required because:

    ○   Shareholders want to be able to sue directors
    ○   Stock markets do not trust financial statements
    ○   Management need encouragement to act in the best interests of all stakeholders
    ○   Companies do not always behave ethically

2   Shareholder activism means:

    ○   The level of shareholder activity within the stock market generally
    ○   The level of involvement shareholders have in the running of a company
    ○   The likelihood of shareholders bringing unethical directors to account
    ○   The balance of power between shareholders and directors

3   The agency problem arises from the fact that there is separation of ownership and management in a company.

    Which of the following is an agent of the company?

    ○   The company's bank
    ○   The company's shareholders acting as a single body
    ○   The company's Board of Directors
    ○   The company's suppliers acting as a single body

4   Which of the following describes corporate governance?

    ○   The system by which companies are directed and controlled
    ○   The duties placed on the Board of Directors by the stock exchange
    ○   Regulations by which shareholders can hold directors to account for their actions
    ○   The concept that directors must act in a socially responsible manner

5   Which of the following are examples of the benefits that corporate governance rules bring to stakeholders?

    Select all that apply.

    ☐   Increased profitability due to fewer mistakes being made
    ☐   Reducing risk to all stakeholders
    ☐   Improving transparency surrounding how the organisation is run
    ☐   Imposing certain checks and controls on directors
    ☐   Improved retention rates of key employees

6   Which type of organisations are owned and democratically controlled by the members who buy those organisation's goods and services?

    ○   Public sector organisations
    ○   Charities
    ○   Partnerships
    ○   Co-operatives

BPP LEARNING MEDIA

7 'The views of the chair on good governance and culture should be communicated'.

Which of CIMA's five proposals for better reporting of corporate governance does this describe?

- ○ How the board works as a team
- ○ Communication and engagement with shareholders
- ○ Tone from the top
- ○ Board effectiveness

8 Who is responsible for the corporate governance of an organisation?

- ○ The Board of Directors
- ○ The Audit Committee
- ○ The shareholders
- ○ The stock exchange

9 Corporate governance rules are designed to benefit a company's stakeholders. Which of the following best describes stakeholders?

- ○ The shareholders
- ○ Those with an interest in the company's financial performance
- ○ All those who are affected by the company's activities both directly and indirectly
- ○ Those who contribute to the success of the company

10 Which THREE of the following are examples of corporate governance?

☐ Internal controls to protect a company's assets

☐ The Board of Directors providing employees with a mission statement

☐ Stock exchange rules that dictate when shareholders may buy and sell shares

☐ An employee performance related pay scheme

☐ CIMA's Fundamental Principles

11 Which of the following correctly describes the purpose of the OECD principles of corporate governance?

- ○ To provide a framework of rules that all businesses must follow
- ○ To lay down informal guidelines that businesses may choose to follow
- ○ To act as a benchmark to ensure that national codes all comply with generally accepted best practice
- ○ To act as an aspiration for the development of future corporate governance codes

12 Which of the following is NOT one of IFAC's drivers for sustainable organisational success?

- ○ Financial management
- ○ Operational excellence
- ○ Effective and transparent communication
- ○ Avoidance of change

13 Which of the following is one of CIMA's suggestions for an improvement to global corporate governance codes?

      ○   Including more specific reports on governance in the Chairman's statement
      ○   Demonstrating how the board works as individuals
      ○   Linking the activities of the board to their remuneration
      ○   Communication with shareholders to be limited to announcements on the company's website

14 Which TWO of the following are common themes of corporate failure due to poor governance?

      ☐   Effective stakeholder interactions
      ☐   Dominant board members
      ☐   Strong internal controls
      ☐   Lack of interest by investment institutions

15 In connection to the corporate agency problem, which of the following is the principal?

      ○   The company itself
      ○   The company's employees
      ○   The company's bank
      ○   The company's directors

5 Governance for corporations

1 What structure does the UK Corporate Governance Code recommend for remuneration committees of large companies?

      ○   Mainly executive directors
      ○   Mainly non-executive directors
      ○   Equal numbers of executive and non-executive directors
      ○   There should be at least three non-executive directors

2 Performance bonuses for directors should only adversely affect a company if:

      ○   The bonuses are paid in cash.
      ○   The bonuses are in the form of shares.
      ○   Directors make short-term decisions to achieve them.
      ○   Directors have to improve a company's share price to achieve them.

3 Which UK report on corporate governance focussed on the role of non-executive directors (NEDs)?

      ○   Higgs
      ○   Tyson
      ○   Greenbury
      ○   Turnbull

BPP
LEARNING
MEDIA

4   Which of the following statements concerning the UK Corporate Governance Code are incorrect?

Select all that apply.

☐ Listed companies must state in their accounts that they complied or did not comply with the code.

☐ No director should be involved in setting their own pay.

☐ Non-compliance with the code creates a civil liability that the directors may be sued for.

☐ Non-compliance with the code may result in the directors being liable for wrongful trading.

☐ Directors of non-compliant companies may be disqualified from acting as a director for up to 5 years.

5   What structure does the UK Corporate Governance Code recommend for audit committees of large companies?

○ Mainly non-executive directors
○ Mainly executive directors
○ The committee should be equally balanced between executive and non-executive directors
○ At least three non-executive directors

6   The King Report on Corporate Governance is which country's approach to corporate governance?

○ USA
○ UK
○ South Africa
○ Australia

7   Noelle is an executive director for a listed, public limited company that is in the FTSE 100 companies and has received several offers of executive directorships in other FTSE 100 companies. She is considering accepting one or more of these offers, as she is confident that she can balance them and her existing directorship.

In order to comply with the UK Corporate Governance Code, how many of those offers of executive directorships can she accept?

○ None
○ One
○ Two
○ Three

8   What best practice does the UK Corporate Governance Code recommend regarding the roles of Chairman and Chief Executive?

○ The Chairman must previously have been the Chief Executive.
○ The Chairman and Chief Executive roles should ideally not be performed by one individual.
○ The Chairman should not have previously been Chief Executive.
○ The Chairman and Chief Executive roles should be combined if possible.

9   Which of the following is a corporate governance measure introduced by the Sarbanes–Oxley Act?

  ○ If a company's financial statements need to be restated, then the CEO and CFO must repay any bonuses received in the last 2 years

  ○ Senior audit partners must be rotated after working on a client for 3 years

  ○ The private company oversight board was established to enforce professional standards in audit and accounting

  ○ Companies must have an audit committee in order to trade

10 Which of the following is the most common board structure for UK companies?

  ○ Single (unitary) board
  ○ Two tier board
  ○ Three tier board
  ○ Joint supervisory and management board

11 What THREE benefits do non-executive directors bring to a board?

  ☐ They bring experience and knowledge into the business that the executive directors may not possess.

  ☐ They will support the Chairman by pushing through their ideas when other directors challenge them.

  ☐ They can appreciate the wider perspective when the executive directors become involved in complex, operational issues.

  ☐ They ensure the executive directors cannot defraud the company.

  ☐ They provide the executive directors someone to confide in regarding any concerns they have with other board members.

12 Which of the following is NOT a board committee suggested by the UK Corporate Governance Code?

  ○ Audit
  ○ Investment
  ○ Nomination
  ○ Remuneration

13 Which THREE of the following are sections of the King Code of Governance Principles?

  ☐ Governance of risk
  ☐ Governance of IT
  ☐ Remuneration committees
  ☐ Integrated reporting and disclosure
  ☐ External audit

14   Which of the following describes the impact of corporate governance on directors' powers and duties?

    ○   Corporate governance has completely replaced the law on directors' powers and duties.   .
    ○   Corporate governance adds additional duties on top of what already exists.
    ○   Corporate governance provides rules that companies can choose to follow instead of the law.
    ○   Corporate governance has had no impact on directors' duties and powers.

15   According to the UK Corporate Governance Code, what is the title given to the non-executive director to whom shareholders can contact outside of the normal channels of communication?

    ○   Director of communications
    ○   Senior independent director
    ○   Compliance officer
    ○   Company secretary

6 The role of audit

1   Which of the following statements about internal audit is true?

    ○   Internal audit is an independent appraisal activity.
    ○   Internal audit is separate from the organisation's internal control system.
    ○   Internal audit is carried out solely for the benefit of the organisation's shareholders.
    ○   The internal audit function reports to the Finance Director.

2   Which of the following statements about external auditors is NOT correct?

    ○   External auditors are appointed by the shareholders of a company.

    ○   The primary responsibility of external auditors is to investigate financial irregularities and report them to shareholders.

    ○   External auditors may rely on the work of internal auditors, if they first assess its worth.

    ○   External auditors are concerned with the financial records and statements of the organisation.

3   In the context of audit, what are 'substantive tests' designed to accomplish?

    ○   To establish whether internal controls are being applied as prescribed
    ○   To identify errors and omissions in financial records
    ○   To establish the causes of errors or omissions in financial records
    ○   To establish an audit trail

4   The susceptibility of a transaction or balance to material misstatement is known as:

    ○   Control risk
    ○   Audit risk
    ○   Inherent risk
    ○   Detection risk

5   The auditors' report on a company's financial statements is expressed in terms of truth and fairness.

Which of the following are generally taken to mean that the financial statements fulfil the requirement of truth and fairness?

Select all that apply.

☐   Free from error

☐   Factual

☐   Free from bias

☐   Free from intellectual dispute

☐   Reflect the commercial substance of the business' transactions

---

6   Materiality is often described as the level of error at which a reader's view of a set of financial statements changes. A common benchmark for materiality is a particular percentage of profit after tax.

Which of the following percentages of profit after tax is the minimum to be classed as material according to the common benchmark?

○   0.5%
○   2%
○   4%
○   6%

---

7   According to CIMA's publication "Fraud risk management: a guide to good practice" what percentage of their annual turnover may organisations be losing to fraud?

○   1%
○   3%
○   5%
○   7%

---

8   The role of internal audit extends beyond auditing the integrity of financial controls and may encompass tasks that add value to the organisation.

Which of the following is an audit of how to improve the economy, efficiency and effectiveness of operations?

○   IT audit
○   Operational audit
○   Value for money audit
○   Procurement audit

9   Internal audit has a role to play in non-financial monitoring and control activities and as such provides a service to an organisation's management. Once the investigation is complete, a report will be submitted that sets out what was found.

Which of the following elements of the report defines the scope of the investigation?

- ○   Executive summary
- ○   Appendix
- ○   Terms of reference
- ○   Conclusion and recommendations

10   Which type of error arises during the recording or posting of a transaction that has taken place?

- ○   Commission
- ○   Principle
- ○   Omission
- ○   Authorisation

11   For a fraud to occur, which THREE of the following must be in place?

- ☐   Flexibility
- ☐   Dishonesty
- ☐   Motive
- ☐   Bias
- ☐   Opportunity

12   Which THREE of the following will help prevent fraud occurring?

- ☐   Segregation of duties
- ☐   Reconciliations
- ☐   Control accounts
- ☐   Authorisation of password sharing
- ☐   Removal of credit control limits for longstanding customers

13   Lothar works in the HR department of a large organisation. Recently an employee left the business, but Lothar did not update the payroll system correctly and was able to collect the non-existent employee's salary himself.

Which type of fraud did Lothar commit?

- ○   Stealing assets
- ○   Ghost employee
- ○   Collusion with third parties
- ○   Manipulation of financial statements

14 Which of the following statements describes an element of internal audit rather than external audit?

- O Responsible to the company's management
- O Opinion on truth and fairness
- O Follows professional standards and regulations
- O Testing is the main activity

15 Which of the following is an example of a test of control?

- O Examining material journal entries

- O Reconciling the financial statements to the underlying accounting records

- O Re-performing transactions

- O Testing large volumes of predictable data by developing an expected balance, comparing to the actual data and reconciling any material differences

7 The importance of CSR

1 The G4 Sustainability Reporting Guidelines sets out three categories of corporate social responsibility that they can report on.

Which of the following lists all three of the categories?

- O Social, legal, ethical
- O Environmental, legal, economic
- O Economic, environmental, social
- O Ethical, environmental, economic

2 Corporate social responsibility has a number of impacts on a firm's operations. The ability of the end-user to recycle or dispose of a product safely would have been considered in which of the following areas of operations?

- O Outbound logistics
- O Quality management
- O Process design
- O Product design

3 Which of the following are included in the OECD's principles on corporate social responsibility?

Select all that apply.

☐ Respect human rights

☐ Encourage local capacity building

☐ Abstain from involvement in local political activities

☐ Accept exemptions not contemplated in the regulatory framework related to environmental, health, safety, labour, taxation, financial incentives, or other issues

☐ Encourage human capital formation

4   Which of the following is one of the International Integrated Reporting Council's seven guiding principles which support the preparation of an integrated corporate report?

- ○   Confidentiality
- ○   Accessibility
- ○   Materiality
- ○   Full disclosure

5   In order to maximise the brand benefits of investments in corporate social responsibility (CSR), three alternative approaches are available.

Which THREE of the following are those approaches?

- ☐   Selective
- ☐   Process
- ☐   Integrated
- ☐   Broadbrush
- ☐   Invisible

6   Which of the following is the name of the international agreement linked to the United Nations Framework Convention on Climate Change, which commits its parties by setting internationally binding emission reduction targets?

- ○   Toronto protocol
- ○   Lisbon protocol
- ○   Beijing protocol
- ○   Kyoto protocol

7   The integrated reporting framework identifies six capitals to assess value creation.

Which of the following is NOT one of the six capitals?

- ○   Virtual
- ○   Financial
- ○   Intellectual
- ○   Natural

8   The triple-bottom line is an important consideration for business operations and requires three things to be delivered simultaneously.

What are the three aspects of the triple-bottom line?

- ○   Human capital, natural capital and intellectual capital
- ○   Economic prosperity, social justice and environmental quality
- ○   Natural capital, social justice and economic prosperity
- ○   Environmental quality, human capital and intellectual capital

9   Which approach to brand management of corporate social responsibility (CSR) states that CSR plays an important and philosophical role in guiding a company but is understated in external communications and initiatives?

○   Invisible
○   Selective
○   Process
○   Integrated

10   Which international body issued extensive guidance to multinational companies on how they should develop policies that take into account the countries in which they operate and the views of other stakeholders?

○   ICC
○   UN
○   OECD
○   ISO

11   CIMA and AICPA produced a joint report "Evolution of corporate sustainability practices" which sets out ten elements of organisational sustainability that are crucial to embedding sustainability into an organisation.

Which of the following is NOT one of the ten elements?

○   Excluding sustainability targets from appraisals
○   Integrating sustainability drivers into strategy
○   Sustainability training
○   Board and senior management commitment

12   Carrol identified four ways that an organisation can respond to social pressures. One of the responses is to voluntarily go beyond what is expected of the organisation.

Which of the four responses does this describe?

○   Defence
○   Proaction
○   Accommodation
○   Reaction

13   Oil, gas and coal are examples of which type of capital?

○   Manufactured
○   Intellectual
○   Natural
○   Financial

14   Which of the following is a possible consequence for a company that adopts a policy of corporate social responsibility (CSR) in its supply chain?

○   Higher disposal costs for waste
○   Increased use of electricity and power
○   Attracting ethical employees
○   Decreased dividends payable to shareholders

15   A company's policy of corporate social responsibility (CSR) is often a source of conflict between stakeholder groups. A company is considering a CSR policy that will see the pay of employees increased.

This policy may cause a conflict between the employees and which other stakeholder group?

O   Shareholders
O   Suppliers
O   Government
O   Debt investors

8 Contract formation 1

1   Which of the following contracts is a standard form contract?

O   An oral agreement between two parties who have negotiated terms regarding the standards of performance to be met by each party in the main contract.

O   An oral agreement to enter into relations on the basis of conditions and warranties as agreed following negotiations between the parties.

O   A document signed by both parties to a contract in which contractual conditions and warranties as negotiated between them are set down.

O   A document put forward for the customer's signature by a supplier of goods in which pre-printed contractual conditions and warranties are set out.

2   Which of the following statements about the law of contract is correct?

O   Providing an agreement is in writing, it will always form a valid contract.

O   Cases involving breach of contract are normally heard in the Crown Court.

O   An agreement between two parties to undertake a criminal act is not a legally recognised contract.

O   An agreement between two businesses to allow late payment for goods or services is not an example of a contract.

3   Petra wishes to sell her car, so places a note in the rear window stating:

'Car for sale $5,000. Call Petra on 01234 456891 if you are interested.'

Which of the following correctly describes the legal nature of Petra's notice?

O   Invitation to tender
O   Offer
O   Invitation to treat
O   Counter offer

4   Ali posted a letter of offer to Muhammed on the 5th June. Muhammed received the letter on the 7th June, and replied via email on the 8th June. The email transmission was delayed and it arrived on the 9th June

On which of the following dates did the parties form an agreement?

- O   5th June
- O   7th June
- O   8th June
- O   9th June

5   What does 'subject to contract' mean in contract law?

- O   The parties are bound by a legally binding contract
- O   The parties have just begun contract negotiations, but no offer has been made
- O   The parties are in contract negotiations, an offer has been made but it has not yet been accepted
- O   The parties have formed an agreement but are still negotiating so are not legally bound

6   Which of the following are essential requirements of a contract?

- (i)   Offer and acceptance
- (ii)   Consideration
- (iii) Written contractual terms
- (iv) Intention to create legal relations

- O   (i), (ii), (iii) and (iv)
- O   (i), (ii) and (iii)
- O   (i), (ii) and (iv)
- O   (i), (iii) and (iv)

7   Which of the following statements concerning the law and contracts is correct?

- O   It is up to the parties to decide if communication of acceptance is required.
- O   Acceptance can be via silence.
- O   Silently nodding your head to bid at an auction could be a form of acceptance.
- O   The postal rules of acceptance do not apply to emails.

8   Which of the following is NOT an essential element of a valid simple contract?

- O   The contract must be in writing.
- O   The parties must be in agreement.
- O   Each party must provide consideration.
- O   Each party must intend legal relations.

9   Simon is keen to buy some second-hand golf clubs. His friend, Dave, advises him to talk to Lee, who is trying to sell a set. Lee tells Simon that he will sell his set for £250. Simon is unsure, because the golf clubs are better and more expensive than he intended buying. He asks Lee if he can tell him in a couple of days. Lee agrees.

Two days later, Simon rings Dave to discuss whether or not to buy the golf clubs. Dave tells him that Lee has changed his mind about selling them. Simon rings Lee up straight away and agrees to buy the clubs for £250.

Is there a contract?

- ○ Yes, because Lee has promised to keep the offer open.
- ○ No, because Simon's request to keep the offer open for a couple of days was too vague to be binding.
- ○ No, because Dave has told Simon of Lee's intentions and the offer has been revoked.
- ○ Yes, because Lee needed to tell Simon himself that he wasn't going to sell the clubs any more.

10 Karl is interested in buying Marcus's car. Marcus is in trouble with his creditors and so is keen to sell. In the course of correspondence, Marcus refuses Karl's offer of £3,000 but states that 'for a quick sale, I will accept £4,000. Please let me know immediately if you are not interested at this price'. Karl accepted this price verbally which Marcus acknowledged.

Later, Marcus, having come into some money, denies that he has made an offer, but that he was providing information about acceptable prices to Karl.

What is the legal position?

- ○ Marcus was only providing information to Karl about prices and this does not constitute an offer for the purposes of contract.

- ○ In the context, it was clear that Marcus was making an offer of sale for that price, which Karl has accepted, so they have a valid contract.

- ○ In the context, it was clear that Marcus was making an offer of sale for that price; however, Karl's acceptance was only verbal and therefore not valid, so they have not got a contract.

- ○ Marcus has made an offer and Karl has accepted, so they have a contract, but Marcus can avoid the contract because Karl has not yet provided the consideration of £4,000.

11 Jude goes into a shop and sees a price label for £200 on a dishwasher. She agrees to buy the dishwasher but the till operator tells her that the label is misprinted and should read £300. Jude maintains that she only has to pay £200.

How would you describe the price on the price label in terms of contract law?

- ○ An acceptance
- ○ An invitation to treat
- ○ An offer
- ○ A tender

12 Alexander wrote to Brian and offered to sell him his set of antique cigarette cards for £300. Brian wrote back that he accepted the offer and would pay for them in two instalments of £150.

Is there a contract?

- ○ Yes. There is offer, acceptance and consideration. The contract is valid.
- ○ No. Alexander's letter was not an offer but an invitation to treat.
- ○ No. Until Alexander receives Brian's letter, the acceptance is not valid.
- ○ No. Brian's letter has varied the terms and so is a counter-offer, rejecting Alexander's original offer.

13   Which of the following is an offer?

    ○   An advertisement in the newsagent's window
    ○   An invitation to tender
    ○   An auction bid
    ○   An exhibition of goods for sale

14   A Ltd wrote to B Ltd offering to sell the company specified items of plant and machinery and requiring acceptance of the offer by fax.

    Which of the following is correct?

    ○   The acceptance is complete as soon as the fax is sent by B Ltd.
    ○   The acceptance is complete as soon as A Ltd receives the fax.
    ○   The contract cannot be concluded by fax.
    ○   Acceptance by fax is subject to the 'post rules'.

15   Which of the following statements regarding counter-offers is correct?

    ○   Counter-offers may be accepted by the original offeror.
    ○   Counter-offers do not terminate the original offer.
    ○   A statement that enquires whether alternative terms would be acceptable is a counter-offer.
    ○   A counter-offer is made by the original offeror to the original offeree.

9 Contract formation 2

1   John owes Catherine £26.89. Kathleen, John's mum, agrees to pay Catherine £20 on John's behalf and Catherine accepts it 'in full settlement'. Two weeks later, Catherine requested the remaining £6.89 from John.

    Is she entitled to the money?

    ○   Yes, because part payment does not provide sufficient consideration for a promise to discharge a debt.

    ○   Yes, because a third party cannot absolve others of their liability under a contract.

    ○   No, because part payment by a third party is good consideration for a promise to discharge a debt.

    ○   No, because intervention by a relative was not intended to be a legal act.

2   Consideration:

    (i)   Must be of adequate and sufficient value
    (ii)   Must move from the promisee
    (iii)   May be the performance of an existing contractual duty
    (iv)   Must be provided at the time the contract is made

    ○   (i) only
    ○   (ii) only
    ○   (ii), (iii) and (iv) only
    ○   (iii) and (iv) only

BPP LEARNING MEDIA

3   Which of the following is a correct rule for valid consideration?

   ○   Consideration must pass from the promisee.
   ○   Consideration must be adequate.
   ○   Past consideration is generally valid consideration.
   ○   Executory consideration is generally not valid consideration.

4   Where a party accepts part payment for a debt, they may at a later date request payment of the amount outstanding unless the other party provided extra consideration when making the part payment.

   Which of the following are valid extra consideration for part payment of a debt?

   Select all that apply.

   ☐   Payment in the form of goods rather than cash
   ☐   Payment by a third party rather than the debtor
   ☐   An intention by the debtor to be legally bound by the part payment
   ☐   A guarantee by the debtor to make the payment on the date agreed in the contract

5   Which of the following statements concerning consideration is correct?

   ○   Performance of an existing legal obligation is valid consideration for the promise of additional reward.

   ○   Performance of an existing contractual duty is sufficient consideration for the promise of additional reward.

   ○   Performance of an existing contractual duty to a third party is sufficient consideration for the promise of additional reward.

   ○   Performance of an extra service in addition to an existing contractual duty is not sufficient consideration for the promise of additional reward.

6   Which of the following is true regarding presumptions of intention to create legal relations?

   ○   Parties in social, domestic and family agreements never intend to be legally bound.

   ○   Parties in commercial agreements never intend to be legally bound.

   ○   The presumption in all agreements is that the parties intend to be legally bound.

   ○   Any presumptions in regard to the intention of parties to be legally bound may be refuted and the burden of proof is on the party seeking to escape liability.

7   In the absence of express statements as to whether or not legal relations are intended:

   ○   The courts always assume that legal relations were not intended.
   ○   The courts assume that legal relations were not intended unless they were social arrangements.
   ○   The courts will assume that legal relations were intended unless the parties can prove otherwise.
   ○   The courts assume that legal relations were intended in commercial cases unless proved otherwise.

8   In which of the following arrangements is there a presumption that legal relations are intended?

    ○   An agreement between a holding company and a subsidiary
    ○   A social arrangement
    ○   A promise by a mother to make a gift to her son
    ○   A domestic arrangement

9   Which of the following statements about legal intention is correct?

    ○   Written agreements always have legal intention.
    ○   Verbal agreements can never have legal intention.
    ○   Spouses can never form legally binding agreements.
    ○   Any legal presumption of intention is capable of being rebutted.

10   Which element of a valid contract is affected by misrepresentation?

    ○   Offer
    ○   Acceptance
    ○   Intention
    ○   Consideration

11   Francis buys a table from Matthew for £100, who believes it to be worthless. Francis knows that it is very valuable. Neither party discloses his belief to the other. Later Matthew discovers that Francis has sold the table for £750,000 to another party in good faith.

What is his remedy?

    ○   Rescind the contract, but he is unable to sue for damages.
    ○   Rescind the contract and sue for damages.
    ○   Report Matthew to the police for fraud.
    ○   Matthew has no remedy.

12   A fraudulent misrepresentation renders a contract:

    ○   Valid
    ○   Void
    ○   Voidable
    ○   Illegal

13   Henry agreed to sell his horse to Richard at a given price. When the negotiations were over and the contract formed, Henry told Richard that the horse was sound and 'has a nice personality'. The horse turned out to be vicious and Richard wants to bring an action against Henry.

Richard will fail in his action because Henry's promise that the horse was not vicious was:

    ○   A statement of opinion not fact.
    ○   Made after the original contract, and was not supported by consideration.
    ○   Not relied upon by Richard when buying the horse.
    ○   Merely a boast made by Henry with no legal effect.

14   In respect of misrepresentation, which THREE of the following are correct?

☐ The person entering the contract must have been aware of the statement's existence.

☐ The statement must have been made to the public at large.

☐ It is sufficient that the misrepresentor knows that the statement will be passed on to the other party.

☐ Silence on a matter generally amounts to misrepresentation.

☐ What has been said must be complete enough not to mislead.

15   In relation to misrepresentation, which of the following statements is incorrect?

○   As a general rule silence cannot amount to misrepresentation.

○   The misrepresentee can affirm and claim damages for any losses

○   A person cannot rely on the misrepresentation if it did not induce them to contract.

○   A half-truth may amount to a misrepresentation.

10 Contract terms

1   Which of the following statements is correct?

○   A breach of warranty allows the innocent party to treat the contract as terminated.

○   A breach of warranty terminates the contract if it is the most equitable outcome.

○   A condition is a term fundamental to the contract.

○   A breach of condition automatically terminates the contract.

2   Which of the following statements is incorrect?

○   Contractual terms may be implied by a court to give the contract business efficacy.

○   Contractual terms may be implied by a court to make the contract fair to each party.

○   Contractual terms may be implied by statute.

○   Contractual terms may be implied by trade custom.

3   Which of the following statements concerning contractual terms are correct?

(i)   Terms are usually classified as either conditions or warranties, but some terms may be unclassifiable in this way.

(ii)   If a condition in a contract is not fulfilled the whole contract is said to be discharged by breach.

(iii)   If a warranty in a contract is not fulfilled the whole contract is said to be discharged by breach, but either party may elect to continue with their performance.

(iv)   Terms which are implied into a contract by law are always contractual conditions.

○   (i) and (ii) only

○   (iii) and (iv) only

○   (i), (ii) and (iv) only

○   (i), (ii), (iii) and (iv)

4   Grace and Geoffrey are both opera singers. They have each contracted with Opera Organisers Ltd to attend rehearsals for a week and then appear in the 2 month long run of a new production. Due to illness, Grace did not attend the rehearsals or the opening night but recovered sufficiently to appear by the fourth night. Due to illness, Geoffrey was unable to attend the first 4 days of rehearsals. Opera Organisers Ltd have booked substitutes for both Grace and Geoffrey for the entire run.

What is the legal position?

- ○   Both Grace and Geoffrey are in breach of a condition of their contract and both of their contracts with Opera Organisers are completely discharged.

- ○   Grace is in breach of condition of her contract, but Geoffrey is in breach of warranty only and his contract is not discharged.

- ○   Grace is in breach of warranty and her contract is not discharged, while Geoffrey is in breach of condition, so his contract is discharged.

- ○   Neither Grace nor Geoffrey are in breach of condition. They are both in breach of warranty, so neither contract is discharged.

5   Dee Ltd has broken one of the terms of its contract with E Ltd. If that term is a warranty, which of the following is correct?

- ○   E Ltd may repudiate the contract and sue for damages.
- ○   E Ltd is entitled to sue for damages or to repudiate the contract.
- ○   E Ltd is only entitled to repudiate the contract.
- ○   E Ltd is entitled to damages only.

6   How are express terms incorporated into a contract?

- ○   By a decision of the courts
- ○   By statute law
- ○   By the parties themselves
- ○   By what is customary in the particular trade

7   Which of the following statements regarding contractual terms are correct?

Select all that apply.

- ☐   The principle of freedom of contract states that parties may include in their contract any terms that they see fit.

- ☐   To be valid, a contract must be complete in its terms.

- ☐   Parties may not allow a third party to determine an essential term of the contract.

- ☐   Where a term is classified as a condition, the only remedy to an injured party if it is breached is to claim damages.

8   An innominate term is one that could either be classified as a condition or a warranty.

How is the classification of an innominate term as a condition or a warranty determined?

- ○   By the operation of statute law
- ○   By the offeror
- ○   By the courts
- ○   By the offeree

9   Which of the following statements is correct?

- ○   The courts may imply a term into a contract for reasons of fairness.
- ○   Innominate terms are implied by statute.
- ○   The parties to a contract can expressly agree the terms of a contract.
- ○   Trade custom is a common source of implied terms.

10   Which of the following is NOT a method by which terms enter a contract?

- ○   By statute
- ○   By the courts
- ○   By trade custom
- ○   By charter

11   A breach of which TWO of the following could result in a contract being repudiated?

- ☐   A guarantee term
- ☐   A warranty term
- ☐   A condition term
- ☐   An innominate term

12   Which of the following statements is correct?

- ○   An innominate term will render a contract void if breached.

- ○   A condition of a contract results in an award of damages only if breached a term.

- ○   Where a contract breach leaves the injured party suffering a total loss of economic benefit they can sue for damages and repudiate the contract.

- ○   A breach of a warranty leads to an award of damages designed to punish the breaching party.

13   A term may be implied into a contract:

    (i)   By statute

    (ii)   By trade practice unless an express term overrides it

    (iii)   By the court to provide for events not contemplated by the parties

    (iv)   By the court to give effect to a term which the parties had agreed upon but failed to express because it was obvious

    (v)   By the court to override an express term which is contrary to normal custom

    ○   (ii) and (iii) only
    ○   (i), (ii) and (iv) only
    ○   (i), (iv) and (v) only
    ○   (i), (iii), (iv) and (v) only

14   Cee Ltd has broken one of the terms of its contract with D Ltd. If that term is a condition, which of the following is correct?

    ○   D Ltd is entitled to repudiate the contract only.
    ○   D Ltd can avoid the contract and recover damages.
    ○   D Ltd is entitled to sue for damages only.
    ○   Cee Ltd's directors can be sued for fraudulent trading.

15   Which of the following is a contractual term, the nature of which is NOT known until it has been breached?

    ○   Innominate term
    ○   Warranty
    ○   Classified term
    ○   Condition

11 The employment relationship

1   Which of the following is NOT a duty of the employer?

    ○   To allow an employee time off after the birth of a child
    ○   To provide an itemised pay slip
    ○   To provide references for the employee when the employee seeks other employment
    ○   To take reasonable care of employees

2   Which of the following is a source/are sources of terms of a contract of employment?

    (i)   Custom and practice
    (ii)   A collective agreement between the union and the employer

    ○   (i) only
    ○   (ii) only
    ○   Both (i) and (ii)
    ○   Neither (i) nor (ii)

3   Which of the following statements concerning employers is NOT correct?

    ○   An employer is obliged to provide an employee with a reference.

    ○   An employer must allow trade union officials reasonable paid time off work to perform their trade union duties.

    ○   An employer must provide an employee with a safe working environment.

    ○   Employees with less than 1 month's service are not entitled to receive statutory notice if dismissed.

4   Which of the following is NOT a common law duty of an employer?

    ○   To provide work to those employed as an apprentice.
    ○   To behave responsibly towards employees.
    ○   To provide an itemised payslip.
    ○   To pay reasonable remuneration to employees.

5   Which of the following is NOT a duty of the employee?

    ○   Reasonable competence
    ○   Obedience
    ○   Absence of error in work undertaken
    ○   Personal service

6   In which of the following areas is an employee NOT protected by legislation?

    ○   Dismissal on grounds of competence
    ○   Dismissal on grounds of race
    ○   Dismissal on grounds of disability
    ○   Dismissal on grounds of sex

7   Mick has been employed by Deck Line Ltd for 4 years. He was aware that the company was experiencing trading difficulties but is still shocked to be sent home without notice when Deck Line Ltd is compulsorily wound up. He sues for wrongful dismissal but at the hearing the liquidator proves that he has discovered that Mick has embezzled £20,000 from the company.

Will Mick succeed in his claim?

    ○   Yes. He has been constructively dismissed.

    ○   Yes. He has been wrongfully dismissed without notice and no regard should be paid to the embezzlement discovered later.

    ○   No. The employment contract was frustrated by Deck Line Ltd's liquidation.

    ○   No. Deck Line Ltd was justified in its dismissal of Mick.

8   The employment tribunal has just established that Ken was unfairly dismissed. There has been a breakdown of confidence between Ken and his former employers.

The tribunal is likely to rule for:

- O   Reinstatement
- O   Re-engagement
- O   Compensation
- O   A punitive additional award

---

9   Which of the following reasons justify dismissal as fair?

(i)   An auditor employed by an auditing firm is struck off their professional body's list for malpractice.

(ii)   A person employed as Finance Director and claiming to be a qualified accountant in fact only has a maths GCSE.

(iii)   A nuclear scientist, despite frequent warnings, persistently fails to secure their experiments, thereby causing danger to colleagues.

(iv)   A solicitor's contract with a firm of solicitors is not renewed because the partners plan to wind up the firm.

- O   (i) and (ii) only
- O   (iii) and (iv) only
- O   (i), (ii) and (iii) only
- O   (i), (ii), (iii) and (iv)

---

10   Nick commences employment under a 3-year contract with Adieu Ltd on 1.8.X6. On 30.6.X9 he is given notice that the contract is not to be renewed.

Assuming that he has a case, what claims may he bring against Adieu Ltd?

- O   Wrongful dismissal only
- O   Unfair dismissal only
- O   Redundancy only
- O   Redundancy and unfair dismissal only

---

11   Which of the following have been given the statutory minimum notice period?

Select all that apply.

- ☐   Anne, who worked for 10 years and was given 9 weeks' notice
- ☐   Barry, who worked for 1 week and was summarily dismissed
- ☐   Catherine, who worked for 5 years and was given 2 months' notice
- ☐   David, who has worked for 18 months and was given a week's notice
- ☐   Emily, who worked for 6 months and was given 3 days' notice

BPP
LEARNING
MEDIA

12 Brian has been employed by Wye Ltd for 10 years. His contract of employment states that if either Wye Ltd or Brian wishes to terminate the contract, each party must give the statutory minimum period of notice.

Which of the following is correct?

○   Both Brian and Wye Ltd are entitled to 10 weeks' notice.
○   Brian is entitled to 10 weeks' notice but Wye Ltd is entitled to only 1 week's notice.
○   Brian is entitled to 1 month's notice and Wye Ltd is entitled to 10 weeks' notice.
○   Both Brian and Wye Ltd are entitled to 1 week's notice.

13 The usual remedy for wrongful dismissal is:

○   Damages under common law principles for breach of contract
○   Reinstatement
○   Re-engagement
○   Statutory compensation

14 Which of the following is/are correct?

(i)   A wrongful dismissal cannot also be an unfair dismissal.
(ii)   An unfair dismissal can also be a wrongful dismissal.
(iii)   An unfair dismissal must also be a wrongful dismissal.

○   (i) only
○   (ii) only
○   (iii) only
○   (i), (ii) and (iii)

15 Organisations should set up a disciplinary policy that sets out a number of areas to employees.

Which of the following is NOT covered by a disciplinary policy?

○   The purpose and scope of the policy
○   Disciplinary offences
○   Constructive dismissal policy
○   What to expect in a disciplinary hearing

12 Policies and practices

1   An employee should ensure the health and safety at work of whom?

○   Other employees and themselves
○   Independent contractors
○   Visitors
○   Themselves and all others at the workplace

2   Bill applied for a job in a warehouse, but was unsuccessful because his status as a wheelchair user meant that he was unable to operate the machinery that the company uses.

Katie applied for a job with the same company, but was turned down after the interviewer told her that 'this is no job for a lady'.

Which of the following statements are correct?

Select all that apply.

☐   Bill has been indirectly discriminated against.

☐   The company is legally required to employ a minimum number of disabled people.

☐   Katie has been indirectly discriminated against.

☐   The manager's comments to Katie are discriminatory in nature.

3   In regard to money laundering, the transfer of monies in order to disguise their source is known by which of the following names?

○   Layering
○   Integration
○   Placement
○   Transposition

4   What is the maximum prison term for someone found guilty of laundering money?

○   8 years
○   10 years
○   14 years
○   16 years

5   The culmination of money laundering activities, giving the money the appearance of being from a legitimate source, is known by which of the following names?

○   Layering
○   Integration
○   Placement
○   Transposition

6   Which of the following statements in relation to the offence of bribery is correct?

○   Bribery is a tort.
○   Bribery can only be committed in the UK.
○   It is an offence for a corporation to fail to prevent bribery.
○   There are no exceptions to the law on bribery.

7   For a disclosure to be a qualifying disclosure under the Public Interest Disclosure Act 1998, it must be made in good faith and which TWO of the following?

☐ There is reasonable belief that it is substantially true

☐ There is reasonable belief that it is accurate

☐ There is reasonable belief that no one will suffer detriment from the disclosure

☐ There is reasonable belief that it is being made to the right person

8   Which of the following is an example of a facilitation payment?

○ A payment made to an official to perform a routine function
○ A payment made to acquire shares on a stock exchange
○ A payment made in return for an illegal service performed
○ A payment made during the money laundering process

9   Which of the following is NOT classified as bribery under the Bribery Act 2010?

○ An individual who accepts payment to perform a public duty.

○ A company that offers a client reasonable hospitality.

○ An employee of a company who offers a non-financial reward to a public official to perform a public duty.

○ A foreign national who works overseas for a company registered in the UK that offers cash to a third party for them to influence a public official.

10 LT is an accountant who works for Tapa Ltd, a company owned by SP. LT has devised a scheme where Tapa Ltd can illegally disguise certain revenues so that the company's tax charge is reduced. Any tax that the scheme saves is paid to SP as a dividend.

Which TWO offences has LT committed?

☐ Tipping off
☐ Failure to prevent
☐ Laundering
☐ Failure to report

11 Which TWO of the following are valid defences available to a charge of bribery?

☐ The person did not expect to make a profit.

☐ The person was exercising their function as a member of the intelligence service.

☐ The person was exercising their function as a member of the armed forces on active service.

☐ The person had reasonable grounds for their conduct.

12 Which of the following is data protection legislation primarily designed to protect?

○ All private individuals and corporate entities on whom only regulated data is held
○ All private individuals on whom only regulated data is held
○ All corporate entities on whom only regulated data is held
○ All private individuals on whom any data is held

13   Which THREE of the following are principles of data protection?

☐   Data must be processed lawfully.

☐   Data can be processed for any purpose.

☐   Data can be freely transferred between countries

☐   Data should be accurate.

☐   Data should be relevant.

14   Which of the following is NOT an offence under the Bribery Act?

○   Bribing another person
○   Bribing a foreign public official
○   Individual managers failing to prevent bribery
○   Receiving a bribe

15   Under the Public Interest Disclosure Act (PIDA) 1998 an employee is protected from dismissal and detriment if they make a qualifying disclosure about their employer.

Which of the following disclosures is NOT a qualifying disclosure under the Act?

○   That a criminal offence has been committed

○   That the directors of the company are being paid excessively

○   That a person has failed, is failing or is likely to fail to comply with any legal obligation to which they are subject

○   That a miscarriage of justice has occurred

13 Legal personality

1   Pepsi and Sheila ran a business together. Whilst the business has been profitable over a number of years they remain cautious in their dealings as they are aware that if things go badly they could both be personally liable.

What type of business entity are Pepsi and Sheila operating?

○   Sole tradership
○   Partnership
○   Private limited company
○   Public limited company

2   Which of the following is an advantage of trading via a partnership?

○   Limited liability of the members
○   Disclosure and audit requirements
○   Veil of incorporation exists
○   Transferability of shares

3   Which of the following is NOT a situation in which the court will 'lift the veil of incorporation'?

○   Where the members or directors are using the veil to evade their legal obligations

○   Where the directors are in breach of the regulations governing the giving of financial assistance for the purchase of the company's own shares

○   Where a quasi-partnership relationship has broken down

○   Where a group of companies has been operating as a single economic entity

---

4   Which of the following is a consequence of the corporate veil?

○   Company cannot enter into contracts in its own name
○   Company cannot own its own property
○   Management and ownership are combined
○   Company can be sued in its own name

---

5   Which of the following are reasons for lifting the corporate veil?

Select all that apply.

☐   Fraudulent trading

☐   Company is being used to shield the owners from the debts of the business

☐   Company is being used to evade legal obligations

☐   When it is reasonable to do so

---

6   Which TWO of the following are true of organisations that have been incorporated?

☐   The maximum number of members is limited

☐   The organisation's liability is limited

☐   The principle of perpetual succession applies

☐   The organisation can use floating charges when borrowing

---

7   Which of the following statements concerning the capacity of a company to contract is correct?

○   A company can enter into a contract only if members pass a resolution permitting it.
○   A company has full capacity to enter into contracts but cannot sue and be sued on them.
○   A company has full capacity to enter into contracts and can sue and be sued on them.
○   A company is not permitted to enter into contracts.

---

8   Which THREE of the following are characteristics of limited companies?

☐   Perpetual succession

☐   Limited liability of the business organisation

☐   Shares may not be sold publicly

☐   Separate legal entity

☐   Limited liability of members

9   Which of the following is/are correct?

    (i)   A company is owned by its shareholders and managed by its directors.

    (ii)   A company is entitled to own property in its own name.

    (iii)   If business is carried on through a company limited by shares, the shareholders can never incur personal liability over and above the amount due on their shares even if the veil of incorporation is lifted.

    ○   (i) only
    ○   (i) and (ii) only
    ○   (i) and (iii) only
    ○   (i), (ii) and (iii)

10   Which THREE of the following are advantages of operating as a sole trader?

    ☐   No requirement to file accounts
    ☐   All the profit accrues to the owner
    ☐   The business is liable for all business debts
    ☐   More control over the business than a company
    ☐   Easier to raise finance

11   Gill wishes to trade but is concerned about losing her house in the event of insolvency. Which of the following entities would best suit Gill in the circumstances?

    ○   A private limited company
    ○   A sole tradership
    ○   An unlimited company
    ○   A partnership

12   Ton Ltd is a wholly owned subsidiary of MBI plc. Fred supplied goods on credit to Ton Ltd, knowing that it was part of the prosperous MBI group. Ton Ltd ran into trading difficulties and is now insolvent. Fred's legal remedy for recovery of his unpaid debt lies against:

    ○   MBI plc
    ○   The directors of Ton Ltd
    ○   The directors of MBI Ltd
    ○   Ton Ltd

13   Krystle was formerly employed by Dynasty Ltd. She has entered into a covenant not to compete with Dynasty Ltd. The covenant is reasonable and not in restraint of trade. Krystle has formed a company, Krystle (Services) Ltd, which has started to trade in competition with Dynasty Ltd. Will Dynasty Ltd be able to get an injunction to prevent Krystle (Services) Ltd from trading?

    ○   No, because Krystle (Services) Ltd has a separate legal identity.
    ○   Yes, because the company has been formed as a device to mask Krystle's carrying on of the trade.
    ○   No, because a company is not liable for the actions of its shareholders.
    ○   Yes, because Krystle (Services) Ltd is engaging in fraudulent trading.

14   Which of the following are statutory grounds for lifting the veil of incorporation?

(i)   Failing to disclose the company's full name on company documents
(ii)   Fraudulent or wrongful trading
(iii)   To identify the controlling mind of a company in cases of corporate manslaughter
(iv)   A listed company carrying on business contrary to the UK Corporate Governance Code

○   (i) and (ii) only
○   (ii) and (iv) only
○   (i), (ii) and (iii) only
○   (i), (ii) and (iv) only

15   Which TWO of the following are advantages of running a business via a company limited by shares?

☐   Increased disclosure

☐   Costs of administration

☐   Separate legal personality

☐   Transferability of ownership

14 Company formation and constitution

1   Which of the following changes must always be made to an off the shelf company when it is purchased from a formation agent?

○   Changing its register of members
○   Restricting its objects
○   Changing its articles
○   Changing its name

2   Which of the following is NOT a feature of a company purchased 'off-the-shelf'?

○   Negatively affects the company's reputation
○   May be cheaper and simpler than incorporating yourself
○   Company is able to trade immediately
○   Company can enter into contracts immediately

3   Which of the following statements relating to a company's articles of association are correct?

Select all that apply.

☐   The articles of association set out the regulations governing the internal conduct of the company.

☐   The articles of association are registered with the Registrar of Companies after the Registrar has issued a certificate of incorporation.

☐   The articles of association are required for a public company, but not for a private company.

☐   The articles of association must state the company's name.

4   Which of the following types of company must obtain a trading certificate from the Registrar of Companies before it can commence trading?

- O   Companies limited by guarantee
- O   Unlimited companies
- O   Public limited companies
- O   Private limited companies

5   Which TWO of the following are regulated by the Articles of Association?

- ☐   Directors' remuneration
- ☐   Issue of shares
- ☐   Members' rights
- ☐   Appointment and dismissal of auditors

6   Which of the following does NOT need to be submitted to the Registrar to form a new company?

- O   Names of the first shareholders
- O   Registration fee
- O   Name of the company
- O   Articles of Association

7   A company's constitution binds which of the following?

- (i)   The company
- (ii)   Members
- (iii)   Third parties

- O   (i) and (ii) only
- O   (i) and (iii) only
- O   (ii) and (iii) only
- O   (i), (ii) and (iii)

8   How long must public limited companies hold their accounting records for?

- O   1 year
- O   3 years
- O   6 years
- O   9 years

9   Which of the following is true of model articles of association?

- O   Model articles of association describe how the company is to be managed and administered.
- O   A company must only use the model articles of association that is relevant to its type of company.
- O   The content of model articles of association cannot be amended by the members.
- O   Model articles of association are created through the application of common law.

BPP
LEARNING
MEDIA

10   Which of the following statements concerning the audit requirements for private and public limited companies is correct?

    ○   Public limited companies must always be audited, private limited companies are exempt from audit

    ○   Public and private limited companies are only required to be audited if they meet certain financial criteria

    ○   Public limited companies must be audited, private limited companies are only required to have an audit if they meet certain financial criteria

    ○   Public and private limited companies are only required to have an audit if the members request one

11   A company can trade in its own name on what date?

    ○   The date the Articles are submitted
    ○   The date that the relevant documents are submitted to the Registrar
    ○   At a date nominated by the first Directors and Shareholders
    ○   The date of the certificate of incorporation

12   Which of the following statements is true concerning a company's Articles of Association?

    ○   They regulate the affairs of the partners
    ○   They regulate the payment of bonuses
    ○   They can be drafted by the company itself
    ○   They cannot be altered

13   This type of company may be allowed to drop the word 'Limited' from its name.

Which of the following entities is being described above?

    ○   A public limited company
    ○   A unlimited company
    ○   A company limited by guarantee
    ○   A private limited company

14   Which TWO of the following are included in the content of a company's model articles of association?

    ☐   Payment of dividends
    ☐   Payment of charitable donations
    ☐   Formation of a remuneration committee
    ☐   Appointment of directors

15   Which of the following is true regarding the content of model articles of association?

    ○   The content of model articles of association is the same for all types of company.

    ○   The content of model articles of association includes clauses relating to the remuneration of employees.

    ○   The content of model articles of association includes clauses relating to the ethical treatment of suppliers.

    ○   The content of model articles of association includes clauses relating to communication with members.

Answers

1 The importance of ethics

1   The correct answer is: Honesty

Leadership requires individuals to promote and respect the other principles. Honesty requires conflicts of interest to be declared. Accountability requires individuals to be responsible for their own actions. Integrity requires the avoidance of actions which could unduly influence decision making.

2   The correct answer is: Enhance the standards of behaviour of members

Codes of practice seek to enhance the standards of behaviour of members. They cannot eliminate unethical behaviour entirely, but they indicate a minimum level of behaviour expected. Codes can be rules based, not just principles based.

3   The correct answer is: It expects members to embody certain principles.

A framework-based approach, such as CIMA's, provides members with guiding principles that they are expected to follow. The other options describe aspects of the rules-based approach to developing a code.

4   The correct answer is: Judgement

Those who follow a framework of fundamental ethical principles must exercise judgement when applying them. The other options are characteristics of the rules-based approach to a code of ethics.

5   The correct answers are:

☐	Policy officer
☑	Compliance officer
☐	Integrity officer
☑	Ethical officer

An ethical (or compliance) officer is responsible for overseeing the application of an organisation's ethical policies and is a point of contact to help employees resolve ethical dilemmas.

6   The correct answers are:

☑	Audit and Assurance Council
☑	Corporate Reporting Council
☐	Corporate Reporting Review Committee
☐	Case Management Committee
☑	Actuarial Council

The Codes and Standards Committee has three separate councils; Audit and Assurance, Corporate Reporting and Actuarial.

The other options form sub-bodies of the Conduct Committee.

7   The correct answer is: Personal principles that guide behaviour

Ethics are personal principles that guide behaviour. They may include aspects of religion or professional guidance, and may include the idea of working together, but this is not necessarily the case.

8   The correct answer is: It attempts to anticipate every possible ethical dilemma.

A rules-based approach attempts to set rules that can be applied in every possible circumstance. The other options describe the framework-based approach to developing a code.

9   The correct answer is: IFAC's code is based on compliance principles.

IFAC's code, like CIMA's, is based on ethical principles (a framework) rather than rules. Such codes require individuals to follow the spirit of the law rather than the letter of the law.

10   The correct answer is: To enhance the quality and standards of services provided by accountants.

IFAC's mission is to enhance the quality of services and to develop high professional standards of accountants. That is why it issued an ethical code.

11   The correct answer is: Egotist

Individuals who seek to maximise their own personal outcomes and to look after their own needs are egotists.

12   The correct answers are:

- ☑ CSC
- ☐ CIMA
- ☑ CC
- ☐ IFAC

The FRC has two bodies: the Codes and Standards Committee (CC) and the Conduct Committee (CC).

13   The correct answer is: Audit quality reviews

The roles of the Conduct Committee include audit quality reviews, corporate reporting reviews, and professional conduct and discipline.

14   The correct answer is: Advising on draft codes and standards

The Codes and Standards Committee advises the FRC on draft codes and standards, and considers and comments on proposed developments relating to international codes and standards.

15   The correct answers are:

- ☑ Discretionary
- ☑ Implicit
- ☑ Prevention
- ☐ Detection
- ☐ Mandatory

Other characteristics of the framework approach include judgement, values driven, principles based, principles (values).

The other options are characteristics of the rules-based approach.

2 CIMA's code of ethics

1   The correct answer is: It can be used to judge the behaviour of members under CIMA's disciplinary procedures.

The code can be used as a basis for judging a member's behaviour against what is expected of them. It does not include legal obligations, is not evidence that all members meet IFAC's criteria and is not required because of CIMA's chartered status.

2   The correct answer is: CIMA's framework is generally the same as IFAC's with some amendments to ensure it meets other regulatory requirements.

Both codes are essentially the same but CIMA's has some adjustments to ensure it fits with local regulations.

3   The correct answer is: Business ethics

According to the CGMA report on responsible business, the application of ethical principles to business behaviour is business ethics. Responsible business involves an organisation operating in an economic, socially and environmentally sustainable way. Ethical performance is the extent to which an organisation's actual performance corresponds to its ethical values and commitments. Ethical management information is quantitative or qualitative information from a range of business sources that allows for the assessment of the organisation's ethical performance.

4   The correct answer is: When requested by a regulator

Requests by a regulator usually require an accountant to disclose confidential information. Requests by a fellow employee, an employer or a client may allow disclosure but the accountant is not obliged to disclose information to them if they do not wish to. Lawyers cannot oblige an accountant to disclose information.

5   The correct answer is: Integrity

Providing misleading information breaches the fundamental principle of integrity.

6   The correct answer is: Respect

Developing relationships and valuing the views and rights of others demonstrates respect. Responsibility means being responsible for your actions. Timeliness means being on time and meeting deadlines. Courtesy means being polite to others.

7   The correct answer is: Accountability

Accountants are accountable for their own judgements and decisions. Independence means avoiding conflicts of interest. Social responsibility means acting in the public interest. Scepticism means questioning information given to you and making your own mind up about it.

8   The correct answer is: Professional competence

An important principle of professional competence is not taking on work if you are not competent to do it. Integrity is about not being party to misleading information. Professional behaviour is the principle of acting in a professional manner with others. Objectivity means to avoid conflicts of interest and protect your independence.

9   The correct answer is: Advocacy threat

Advocacy threats are created when an accountant promotes their client's or employer's position. Familiarity threats result from being too close to the work so you cannot be objective. Self-review threats occur where the accountant is required to review their own work. Intimidation threats are created by third parties putting pressure on the accountant.

10   The correct answers are:

- ☑ Working part-time for two rival businesses
- ☐ Owning shares in a company that competes with your employer
- ☑ Being employed by a close relative
- ☑ Being offered a valuable gift by a friend who is also a business contact
- ☐ Receiving a performance bonus from your manager

Conflicts of interest are created when an accountant's objectivity is questioned. This may occur where they act for two rival business (would one be favoured over the other?), they are employed by a close relative (would they want to cause a rift with the relative?) and they are offered a gift (is it a bribe?). Owning shares in a company that competes with your employer does not create a conflict of interest as you are not in a position to affect its results. The performance bonus would only cause a conflict if you were able to determine if you were eligible.

11   The correct answers are:

- ☐ By keeping their mind free from distractions.
- ☑ By seeking supporting evidence before accepting information is accurate.
- ☑ By investigating why information was given to them.
- ☑ By reviewing the work of a junior before accepting it as correct.
- ☐ By being straightforward and honest at all times.

The correct options demonstrate questioning and non-acceptance that work is correct on face value. Being straightforward and honest demonstrates integrity. Keeping your mind free from distractions demonstrates objectivity.

12   The correct answer is: Professional behaviour

Professional behaviour. Their actions are certainly dishonest and may constitute fraud.

13   The correct answer is: Objectivity
Objectivity is a combination of impartiality, intellectual honesty and a freedom from conflicts of interest.

Integrity is the important principle of honesty and requires accountants to be straightforward in all professional and business relationships.

Confidentiality means to safeguard the security of information unless there is a legal or professional right or duty to disclose. It also means not using information obtained in the course of work for personal advantage or for the benefit of others.

Professional competence and due care means accountants should refrain from performing any services that they cannot perform with reasonable care, knowledge, competence, diligence and a full awareness of the important issues.

14   The correct answer is: Self-interest threat

A self-interest threat is the risk that a financial or other interest may influence the accountant's judgement or behaviour. It is also known as a 'conflict of interest' threat.

An advocacy threat is the risk that an accountant promotes a client's or employer's position to the point that their objectivity is compromised.

A familiarity threat is the risk that due to a long or close relationship with a client or employer, an accountant will be too sympathetic to their interests or too ready to accept their work.

A self-review threat is the risk that an accountant may not appropriately re-evaluate their (or a colleague's) previous work (including judgements made or services performed) when relying on the work while performing a current service.

15   The correct answer is: As the accounting environment is constantly evolving

Lifelong learning ensures an accountant keeps up to date with technical and other skills that are developed and change over time. There is no legal requirement to follow lifelong learning. The level of skills compared to other accountancy bodies and assertiveness development are irrelevant.

3 Ethical dilemmas

1   The correct answer is: Professional and corporate

The manager represents corporate values; accounting standards represent professional values.

2   The correct answer is: Supplying confidential information about the company's financial results in exchange for gifts

Supply of such information for gain amounts to bribery – a criminal offence. The other options are examples of unethical behaviour but are not criminal offences.

3   The correct answers are:

✓	Professional bodies may lose their 'chartered' status
✓	Increased regulation of the profession by external organisations
☐	Increased employability of accountants
☐	Improved reputation of the profession
✓	Reduced public trust in the profession

Professional bodies can lose their 'chartered' status if they are no longer seen to act in the public interest. The profession may be subject to external regulation or legal regulation by government if it cannot regulate itself adequately. The public will lose trust in it. Employability of accountants and the profession's reputation will be damaged if members behave unethically.

4   The correct answer is: Take legal advice before proceeding

Legal advice should always be taken before breaching any duty of confidentiality to minimise any risk of legal action by the affected party. Proceeding with the solution and taking advice from friends and family both involve breaching confidentiality. Not proceeding with the resolution would mean the accountant behaving unethically and being at risk of disciplinary action by CIMA.

5   The correct answer is: The law

The law overrides everything for CIMA students and members. The secondary obligation is to CIMA's Ethical Code.

6   The correct answer is: Confidentiality

Management accounts are for a company's internal use; someone has leaked the results to a member of the public and the Finance Director should not have disclosed the operational reasons for poor performance. There is no breach of objectivity because there is no conflict of interest. Integrity has not been breached because the director has been straightforward and honest. Professional competence is not in question.

7   The correct answer is: The Government

The Government is a financial stakeholder because it collects taxes and social security payments from the company. The other options are stakeholders that do not have a financial interest in the company.

8   The correct answers are:

✓	Check all the facts
✓	Decide if the issue is legal in nature
✓	Identify affected parties
☐	Document their day to day feelings
☐	Seek advice from their families

These are all included in CIMA's ethical checklist. There is no need to record personal feelings. Advice should not be sought from families as this may breach confidentiality.

9   The correct answer is: Cost

Transparency, effect and fairness are three things that an accountant should consider when resolving an ethical issue. Cost is not relevant to such a decision.

10   The correct answer is: Integrity

Integrity is the important principle of honesty and requires accountants to be straightforward in all professional and business relationships. It also means not being party to the supply of false or misleading information. The continued use of estimates risks inaccurate trade receivables and payables and therefore misleading accounts.

Objectivity is a combination of impartiality, intellectual honesty and a freedom from conflicts of interest.

Professional competence and due care means accountants should refrain from performing any services that they cannot perform with reasonable care, knowledge, competence, diligence and a full awareness of the important issues.

11   The correct answer is: Themselves

A CIMA member should always look to resolve the matter themselves before taking it to other parties.

12   The correct answer is: The accountant should follow their professional ethics at the expense of their contractual obligation.

Professional ethics should always be followed even if this means breaking a contractual obligation. This can create a dilemma for an accountant, especially if the professional ethics or directions from their employer conflict with the accountant's professional ethics.

13   The correct answer is: No dilemma

No dilemma. There is no issue of objectivity since the meal is not valuable, has been offered to others, and appears just to be a general goodwill gesture between a supplier and a long-time customer. There is no risk to confidentiality unless the supplier asks for confidential information. As long as you are straightforward and honest there is no risk to integrity.

14   The correct answer is: Yes, a risk of breaking integrity

The main principle being broken is integrity. Sending inaccurate information to the Finance Director makes you party to misinformation.

15   The correct answer is: The law

The law always overrides professional duties and personal ethics.

4 The meaning of corporate governance

1   The correct answer is: Management need encouragement to act in the best interests of all stakeholders

Shareholders do not need corporate governance rules to be able to sue directors. There is no serious mistrust of financial statements by stock markets. Corporate governance rules were developed to help protect stakeholders from corporate collapses, to improve financial reporting and to facilitate the globalisation of investment, not to ensure all companies act ethically.

2   The correct answer is: The level of involvement shareholders have in the running of a company

Shareholder activism relates to the level of involvement a company's shareholders have in running the organisation.

3   The correct answer is: The company's Board of Directors

The Board of Directors is the agent of the company and the shareholders own the company. Banks and suppliers are stakeholders.

4   The correct answer is: The system by which companies are directed and controlled

Corporate governance is defined as the system by which companies are directed and controlled. It is about how companies are run, not how directors are regulated.

5   The correct answers are:

- [ ] Increased profitability due to fewer mistakes being made
- [x] Reducing risk to all stakeholders
- [x] Improving transparency surrounding how the organisation is run
- [x] Imposing certain checks and controls on directors
- [ ] Improved retention rates of key employees

Although corporate governance rules may reduce the number of mistakes being made, it cannot be certain that profitability will improve. It is unlikely that retaining key employees can be achieved purely through following corporate governance rules.

6   The correct answer is: Co-operatives

Co-operatives are owned and democratically controlled by members who buy the organisation's goods and services.

7   The correct answer is: Tone from the top

In CIMA's proposal, tone from the top, the views of the chair on good governance and culture should be communicated.

8   The correct answer is: The Board of Directors

The UK Corporate Governance Code makes it clear that as stewards of a company, responsibility for governance lies with the directors.

9   The correct answer is: All those who are affected by the company's activities both directly and indirectly

Stakeholders are those who the company's activities affect both directly, such as the employees and indirectly, such as the Government.

10   The correct answers are:

- [x] Internal controls to protect a company's assets
- [x] The Board of Directors providing employees with a mission statement
- [ ] Stock exchange rules that dictate when shareholders may buy and sell shares
- [x] An employee performance related pay scheme
- [ ] CIMA's Fundamental Principles

Stock Exchange rules are external rules that apply to the shareholders of a company, and do not affect how the company is run. CIMA's Fundamental Principles apply to CIMA members not businesses. The other options are examples of corporate governance because they affect how the company is run.

11   The correct answer is: To act as a benchmark to ensure that national codes all comply with generally accepted best practice

The purpose behind the OECD principles is that they are to act as a benchmark to ensure that national codes all comply with generally accepted best practice.

12   The correct answer is: Avoidance of change

Far from avoiding change, another one of the drivers is 'innovation and adaption' – adapting the organisation to changing circumstances.

The other drivers are:

Customer and shareholder focus
Effective leadership and strategy
Integrated governance, risk and control
People and talent management

13   The correct answer is: Including more specific reports on governance in the Chairman's statement

One of CIMA's suggestions to improve global corporate governance codes is to include more specific reports on governance in the Chairman's statement.

Other suggestions include:

Demonstrating how the board works as a team

Linking the activities of the board to the key corporate events, using graphics if required to link actions to events

Communication and engagement with stakeholders explained via detailed reporting on how the investor relations were managed

14   The correct answers are:

☐	Effective stakeholder interactions
☑	Dominant board members
☐	Strong internal controls
☑	Lack of interest by investment institutions

Lack of stakeholder interaction and lack of internal controls are correct common themes for failure due to poor governance.

15   The correct answer is: The company itself

In agency, the principal is the party that the agent works for. The company is the principal and the agents are the directors. The others are third parties.

5 Governance for corporations

1   The correct answer is: There should be at least three non-executive directors

The code states that remuneration committees of large companies should consist of at least three non-executive directors.

2   The correct answer is: Directors make short-term decisions to achieve them.

Directors who take short-term decisions in order to obtain a bonus can adversely affect the company if it is not in the long-term interest of the business. The form of payment should not adversely affect a company provided the bonus scheme is correctly set up. By increasing their company's share price, the directors should have improved the financial position of the company, which is to the company's benefit.

3   The correct answer is: Higgs

The Higgs report focused on the role of NEDs. Tyson focused on their recruitment and development. Greenbury focused on director remuneration and Turnbull focused on directors and internal control systems.

4   The correct answers are:

☐	Listed companies must state in their accounts that they complied or did not comply with the code.
☐	No director should be involved in setting their own pay.
☑	Non-compliance with the code creates a civil liability that the directors may be sued for.
☑	Non-compliance with the code may result in the directors being liable for wrongful trading.
☑	Directors of non-compliant companies may be disqualified from acting as a director for up to 5 years.

Non-compliance is not a criminal or civil offence and will not result in disqualification of directors. Listed companies must state in their accounts whether or not they complied with the code.

5   The correct answer is: At least three non-executive directors

According to the UK Corporate Governance Code, audit committees of large companies should include at least three non-executive directors. The Board should also satisfy itself that at least one member of the Audit Committee has recent and relevant financial experience.

6   The correct answer is: South Africa

The King Report is produced in South Africa.

7   The correct answer is: None

According to the UK Corporate Governance Code. Executives should only hold one FTSE 100 board membership.

8   The correct answer is: The Chairman and Chief Executive roles should ideally not be performed by one individual.

The UK Corporate Governance Code recommends a clear division of power so that one person does not have unfettered powers of decision. Therefore the roles of Chairman and Chief Executive should not be performed by one person.

The other options are not best practice suggested by the UK Corporate Governance Code.

9   The correct answer is: Companies must have an audit committee in order to trade

Under SOX, companies must have an audit committee in order to trade. If financial statements are restated then the CEO and CFO must repay bonuses received in the last 12 months. Senior audit partners must be rotated every 5 years. The public company oversight board was established.

10   The correct answer is: Single (unitary) board

In the UK the most common board structure is the single (unitary) board. Dual (management and supervisory) boards are common in Europe. In Japan, three tier boards are commonplace.

11   The correct answers are:

☑   They bring experience and knowledge into the business that the executive directors may not possess.

☐   They will support the chairman by pushing through their ideas when other directors challenge them.

☑   They can appreciate the wider perspective when the executive directors become involved in complex, operational issues.

☐   They ensure the executive directors cannot defraud the company.

☑   They provide the executive directors someone to confide in regarding any concerns they have with other board members.

Non-executive directors should bring experience, knowledge and a wider perspective into the company. They are also there for the executive directors to talk to with any issues they may be having. They bring a strong, independent element on the Board, and are not there to act as 'henchmen' to enable the Chairman to get their own way. Although the presence of non-executive directors may help deter fraud, they will never eliminate it.

12   The correct answer is: Investment

An investment committee was not suggested by the UK Corporate Governance Code. The other options are all recommended by the UK Corporate Governance Code.

13   The correct answers are:

☑   Governance of risk
☑   Governance of IT
☐   Remuneration committees
☑   Integrated reporting and disclosure
☐   External audit

The King Code of Governance principles includes the following nine sections:

Ethical leadership and corporate citizenship, boards and directors, audit committees, governance of risk, governance of IT, compliance with laws, rules, codes and standards, internal audit, governing stakeholder relationships and integrated reporting and disclosure.

14   The correct answer is: Corporate governance adds additional duties on top of what already exists.

Corporate governance does not affect existing statutory and fiduciary duties. Instead, it adds additional duties on top of them, such as the need to engage constructively with shareholders and to manage risk responsibly.

15   The correct answer is: Senior independent director

According to the UK Corporate Governance Code, the title given to the non-executive director to whom shareholders can contact outside of the normal channels of communication is Senior Independent Director.

BPP
LEARNING
MEDIA

6 The role of audit

1   The correct answer is: Internal audit is an independent appraisal activity.

Internal audit is independent, but is still part of the internal control system: it is a control which examines and evaluates the adequacy and efficacy of other controls. Internal auditors should report directly to the Audit Committee of the Board of Directors (in order to preserve independence). It is external audit which is for the benefit of shareholders: internal audit is a service to management.

2   The correct answer is: The primary responsibility of external auditors is to investigate financial irregularities and report them to shareholders.

The primary responsibility of the external auditor is to report to shareholders on whether the client's financial statements are accurate and free from bias ('true and fair'). The other options are true.

3   The correct answer is: To identify errors and omissions in financial records

Substantive tests 'substantiate' the figures in the accounts. They are used to discover whether figures are correct or complete, not why they are incorrect or incomplete, or how the figures 'got there'.

4   The correct answer is: Inherent risk

Inherent risk is the susceptibility of an transaction or balance to material misstatement. Audit risk is the risk that the auditor gives an incorrect opinion on the financial statements. Control risk is the risk that a control would not have prevent a or detected a material misstatement. Detection risk is the risk that the auditor fails to detect a material misstatement.

5   The correct answers are:

☐	Free from error
☑	Factual
☑	Free from bias
☐	Free from intellectual dispute
☑	Reflect the commercial substance of the business' transactions

An audit provides assurance that the financial statements are free from material misstatement not error. The figures and accounting policies included in the accounts may give rise to dispute because different accountants may take a different view of how transactions should be accounted for.

Truth and fairness is based on the principles that the financial statements are factual, free from bias and reflect the commercial substance of the business' transactions.

6   The correct answer is: 6%

According to the common benchmark, a figure between 5% and 10% of profit after tax would be considered material.

7   The correct answer is: 7%

According to CIMA's publication "Fraud risk management: a guide to good practice" organisations may be losing 7% of their annual turnover to fraud.

8   The correct answer is: Value for money audit

A value for money audit is an audit of how to improve the economy, efficiency and effectiveness of operations.

IT audits assess current capability and future flexibility of an organisation's IT systems.

Operational audits assess the effectiveness of management and processes.

Procurement audits assess the effectiveness of purchasing operations.

9   The correct answer is: Terms of reference

Terms of reference define the scope of the investigation. The executive summary is a high-level summary of the report, the appendix contains supporting analysis and the conclusion and recommendations contains the findings of the report and sets out what should be done next.

10   The correct answer is: Commission

Errors of commission arise during the recording or posting of a transaction that has taken place.

Errors of principle occur during the recording a transaction in violation of accounting standards. Errors of omission are either partial or total omission from the books of prime entry. There is no such error as error of authorisation.

11   The correct answers are:

☐	Flexibility
☑	Dishonesty
☑	Motive
☐	Bias
☑	Opportunity

The three elements which must be in place for fraud to occur are dishonesty, motive and opportunity. The other options are not required.

12   The correct answers are:

☑	Segregation of duties
☑	Reconciliations
☑	Control accounts
☐	Authorisation of password sharing
☐	Removal of credit control limits for longstanding customers

Segregation of duties, reconciliations and control accounts are examples of controls that help prevent fraud. Authorisation of password sharing and the removal of credit limits may actually increase the chance of fraud as they remove important controls.

13 The correct answer is: Ghost employee

Collecting payments for employees who don't exist is known as setting up a ghost employee.

Stealing assets involves physically or virtually stealing something. You could argue that Lothar is stealing money, which is an asset, but ghost employee is what the type of fraud Lothar has committed is known as. There is no collusion with a third party in the scenario. There is no manipulation of the financial statements in this scenario.

14 The correct answer is: Responsible to the company's management

Internal audit will do anything the company's management requests and so may perform any activity (not just testing) and will follow any rules or guidelines required. It is ultimately responsible to the company's management.

External audit follows professional standards and regulations to test the company's financial statements in order to form an opinion about their truth and fairness. It is ultimately responsible to the company's shareholders.

15 The correct answer is: Re-performing transactions

Re-performing transactions is an example of a test of control. Examining material journal entries and reconciling financial statements to underlying accounting records are examples of substantive tests. Testing large volumes of predictable data by developing an expected balance, comparing to the actual data and reconciling any material differences describes analytical review.

7 The importance of CSR

1 The correct answer is: Economic, environmental, social

The three categories of the G4 Sustainability Reporting Guidelines are economic, environmental and social.

2 The correct answer is: Product design

The ability of an end-user to recycle or safely dispose of a product would have been determined in product design.

3 The correct answers are:

☑ Respect human rights

☑ Encourage local capacity building

☐ Abstain from involvement in local political activities

☐ Accept exemptions not contemplated in the regulatory framework related to environmental, health, safety, labour, taxation, financial incentives, or other issues

☑ Encourage human capital formation

Respecting human rights, encouraging local capacity building and encouraging human capital formation are all included in the OECD's general policies.

4   The correct answer is: Materiality

Materiality is one of the seven guiding principles. The others are strategic focus and future orientation, connectivity of information, stakeholder relationships, conciseness, reliability and completeness, and consistency and comparability.

5   The correct answers are:

✓	Selective
	Process
✓	Integrated
	Broadbrush
✓	Invisible

The three approaches to maximising the brand benefits of investment in CSR are selective, integrated and invisible. The other options are not known approaches.

6   The correct answer is: Kyoto protocol

The Kyoto protocol is the international agreement linked to the United Nations Framework Convention on Climate Change, which commits its parties by setting internationally binding emission reduction targets.

7   The correct answer is: Virtual

Virtual is not one of the six capitals. The others are manufactured, human, and social and relationship.

8   The correct answer is: Economic prosperity, social justice and environmental quality

The three aspects to the triple-bottom line are economic prosperity, social justice and environmental quality.

9   The correct answer is: Invisible

The invisible approach states that CSR plays an important and philosophical role in guiding a company but is understated in external communications and initiatives. The selective approach states that CSR is developed in certain and specific ways. The integrated approach states that the brand and CSR operate in synchrony. There is no such thing as a process approach.

10   The correct answer is: OECD

The OECD has issued a number of general policies on how multinational companies should develop policies that take into account the countries in which they operate and the views of other stakeholders.

The other options are international organisations, but they did not issue such guidelines.

11   The correct answer is: Excluding sustainability targets from appraisals

One of the ten elements is including sustainability targets in appraisals. The other options are all included in the ten elements of the report.

12   The correct answer is: Proaction

Proaction involves voluntarily going beyond what is expected (such as industry norms). Reaction involves denying responsibility. Defence involves fighting responsibility and then doing the least required to comply. Accommodation involves accepting responsibility and then doing what is expected.

13   The correct answer is: Natural

Natural capital consists of available environmental resources such as oil, gas and coal. Financial capital is the pool of investment funds available to a company. Manufactured capital is the infrastructure available to help the organisation deliver goods and services. Intellectual capital includes intangible assets such as patents and licences.

14   The correct answer is: Attracting ethical employees

Following a policy of CSR should reduce the amount of waste produced and power used by an organisation; therefore these costs should fall. The level of dividends are set by the company's management and are not directly affected by a CSR policy, though evidence suggests that positive CSR can in fact increase a business' profits and dividends. Businesses that become socially responsible do become more attractive to likeminded, ethical employees.

15   The correct answer is: Shareholders

The policy will increase staff costs and therefore reduce the amount of the company's profit available for distribution to shareholders in their dividend.

Suppliers are unaffected by the policy. The Government should receive an increase of income tax from the employees and it will therefore not be a source of conflict. Debt investors are unaffected as they must be repaid despite the level of company profit.

8 Contract formation 1

1   The correct answer is: A document put forward for the customer's signature by a supplier of goods in which pre-printed contractual conditions and warranties are set out.

Standard form contracts are documents that customers complete in order to obtain goods or services from large organisations such as utility companies. They are unlikely to be oral and there is no negotiation because the customer accepts the terms or must choose another supplier.

2   The correct answer is: An agreement between two parties to undertake a criminal act is not a legally recognised contract.

An illegal act cannot form the basis for a valid contract. Just because an agreement is in writing does not mean it will always be a valid contract. The Crown Court does not usually hear civil cases such as contractual disputes. Businesses are usually free to contract on any terms that they wish.

3   The correct answer is: Invitation to treat

Invitation to treat. Vague adverts like this fall short of being an offer, so would be classified as an ITT – it is designed to encourage interested parties to make Petra an offer.

4   The correct answer is: 9th June

9th June. The parties are in agreement when offer and acceptance are completed. In this case acceptance is via email, which is only effective where and when it is received – in this case on the 9th June.

5   The correct answer is: The parties have formed an agreement but are still negotiating so are not legally bound

Subject to contract means that the parties have formed an agreement but are still negotiating so are not legally bound.

6   The correct answer is: (i), (ii) and (iv)

The three essential elements of contract are offer and acceptance (ie agreement), consideration and intention to create legal relations. Some contracts require written terms, but by no means all.

7   The correct answer is: The postal rules of acceptance do not apply to emails.

The postal rules do not apply to instantaneous forms of communication, such as emails. The law decides whether communication is accepted, not the parties, acceptance cannot be via silence. At an auction a nod by a bidder would signal an offer, not acceptance.

8   The correct answer is: The contract must be in writing.

Simple contracts may be oral or implied by conduct. Agreement, consideration and legal intention are all essential elements of a valid simple contract.

9   The correct answer is: No, because Dave has told Simon of Lee's intentions and the offer has been revoked.

Lee's offer has been revoked so there can be no contract. Revocation can be communicated by a reliable third party (as in *Dickinson v Dodds*). In this case, Dave can be seen as a reliable third party, because he has been involved in the process. Simon's request to keep the offer open is irrelevant since Lee is entitled to revoke his offer at any time.

10   The correct answer is: In the context, it was clear that Marcus was making an offer of sale for that price, which Karl has accepted, so they have a valid contract.

Marcus clearly made an offer of £4,000, which Karl accepted. Verbal acceptance is valid if acknowledged. Karl's promise to pay £4,000 is valid consideration for the car.

11   The correct answer is: An invitation to treat

In law, a price label is an invitation to treat. Jude offers to buy at the price stated on the label and the till operator can accept or reject the offer.

12   The correct answer is: No. Brian's letter has varied the terms and so is a counter-offer, rejecting Alexander's original offer.

Alexander's offer to sell the cards for £300 is legally an offer. However, Brian varied the terms of the offer when replying to Alexander by stating the instalment terms. This variation is a counter-offer which rejects Alexander's original offer. Had Brian's reply not been a counter-offer it would be valid when posted and a contract would have been formed.

13   The correct answer is: An auction bid

The others are examples of invitations to treat. A bid made is an offer to buy the item that is being auctioned.

14   The correct answer is: The acceptance is complete as soon as A Ltd receives the fax.

This is similar to the use of a telex in *Entores v Miles Far Eastern Corporation*. The offeree must make sure that their acceptance is received and understood when using any instantaneous method of communication. Contracts can be concluded by fax and the postal rule does not apply.

15   The correct answer is: Counter-offers may be accepted by the original offeror.

Counter-offers have the effect of terminating the original offer, but may be accepted by the original offeror. A statement that enquiries whether alternative terms would be acceptable is a request for information, not a counter-offer. Counter-offers are made by the original offeree to the original offeror.

9 Contract formation 2

1   The correct answer is: No, because part payment by a third party is good consideration for a promise to discharge a debt

Part payment of a debt is sufficient consideration for the full amount of the debt if the lender receives something they were not previously entitled to, such as payment by a third party. Whether the third party is a relative or not is irrelevant.

2   The correct answer is: (ii) only

Consideration need only be sufficient – it need not be adequate. Performance of an existing contractual duty is not good consideration. Consideration does not need to be provided at the time the contact is made as a promise to pay or provide a service is all that is required. Because consideration is the price of a promise, it must be paid by the person who seeks to enforce it and therefore moves from the promisee.

3   The correct answer is: Consideration must pass from the promisee.

Consideration must pass from the promisee. It must be sufficient but not necessarily adequate. Past consideration is generally not valid consideration. Executory consideration is generally valid consideration.

4   The correct answers are:

✓	Payment in the form of goods rather than cash
✓	Payment by a third party rather than the debtor
☐	An intention by the debtor to be legally bound by the part payment
☐	A guarantee by the debtor to make the payment on the date agreed in the contract

For the extra consideration to be valid, the creditor must become entitled to something that they are not already entitled to. In this case, goods rather than cash and payment by a third party are valid examples. A guarantee of payment and payment on time are not valid as extra consideration because the creditor is already entitled to them.

5   The correct answer is: Performance of an existing contractual duty to a third party is sufficient consideration for the promise of additional reward.

The performance of an existing contractual duty or legal obligation is not sufficient consideration for the promise of additional reward unless an additional service is also provided, or if the duty is provided to a third party instead.

6   The correct answer is: Any presumptions in regard to the intention of parties to be legally bound may be refuted and the burden of proof is on the party seeking to escape liability.

Parties in social, domestic and family agreements are presumed not to intend to be legally bound, but this presumption is rebuttable. Parties in commercial contracts are presumed to intend to be legally bound, but this presumption is rebuttable. In regard to rebutting either presumption, the burden of proof is on the party seeking to escape liability.

7   The correct answer is: The courts assume that legal relations were intended in commercial cases unless proved otherwise.

Courts will presume commercial arrangements are intended to be legally binding, but this presumption is rebuttable if proved otherwise. Social or domestic arrangements are presumed not to have been intended to be legally binding, but this presumption is also rebuttable if proved otherwise.

8   The correct answer is: An agreement between a holding company and a subsidiary

Legal relations are presumed in commercial transactions. In domestic and social transactions there is no presumption of legal relations, although this can be established if it can be proved that legal relations were intended. This would not be the case where a gift is made.

9   The correct answer is: Any legal presumption of intention is capable of being rebutted.

With strong evidence to the contrary any of the presumptions about implied legal intention can be rebutted. In *Jones v Vernon Pools* a written agreement was non-binding due to the use of the words 'binding in honour only'. Making a verbal agreement in a commercial capacity will usually lead to a binding contract. The usual presumption of no intention between spouses was overturned in *Merritt v Merritt* where an agreement was made between spouses while they were separating.

10   The correct answer is: Intention

Misrepresentation means that one of the parties to the contract did not genuinely consent to it. Therefore, it is intention that is affected.

11   The correct answer is: Matthew has no remedy.

A misrepresentation would be made by the seller of the goods to the buyer. Francis has no obligation to let Matthew know the table's real value. Therefore there has been no misrepresentation.

12   The correct answer is: Voidable

Where there is misrepresentation, the contract continues unless set aside by the representee. Therefore it is voidable.

13   The correct answer is: Made after the original contract, and was not supported by consideration.

The other options could potentially all be true. It is important to look at the timing of actions in the question to establish the correct answer. In this case the statement was made after the contract, so there was no reliance on the statement, hence no misrepresentation.

14   The correct answers are:

✓	The person entering the contract must have been aware of the statement's existence.
	The statement must have been made to the public at large.
✓	It is sufficient that the misrepresentor knows that the statement will be passed on to the other party.
	Silence on a matter generally amounts to misrepresentation.
✓	What has been said must be complete enough not to mislead.

The statement may have been made to the public at large but there is no requirement for this (such as in an agreement between two individuals). Silence generally does not amount to misrepresentation because neither party is under any duty to disclose what they know. The other options are all correct statements concerning misrepresentation.

15   The correct answer is: The misrepresentee can affirm and claim damages for any losses

Silence cannot generally amount to misrepresentation, but a half-truth can. For a person to rely on the misrepresentation it must have induced them to enter the contract. Misrepresentation makes a contract voidable, but not void. The contract remains valid, and the representee may choose to affirm it. By making this choice, the representee cannot claim damages as well.

10 Contract terms

1   The correct answer is: A condition is a term fundamental to the contract.

Breach of a warranty never terminates a contract. Breach of a condition (a term fundamental to a contract) entitles the innocent party to treat the contract as terminated, but termination is not automatic.

2   The correct answer is: Contractual terms may be implied by a court to make the contract fair to each party.

Terms may be implied by a court, to give business efficacy to a contract, or if allowed by statute and trade custom. However, courts will not interfere to correct a 'bad bargain'.

3   The correct answer is: (i) and (ii) only

Most contractual terms in business agreements are identified as being either conditions or warranties, the importance of the distinction being that failure to fulfil a condition leads to the whole contract being at an end (discharged by breach). However, breach of warranty leads only to a claim for damages, not to discharge.

Terms can be unclassified when the contract is formed. They will be classed as either a condition or warranty once the effects of failure to fulfil it are known and assessed.

Terms implied by statute can be conditions or warranties.

4   The correct answer is: Grace is in breach of condition of her contract, but Geoffrey is in breach of warranty only and his contract is not discharged.

According to the decisions in *Poussard v Spiers* and *Bettini v Gye*, failure to sing on an opening night breaks a condition of the contract and discharges it. Missing rehearsals does not and is just a breach of a warranty.

5   The correct answer is: E Ltd is entitled to damages only.

In contract law, breach of a warranty entitles the injured party to claim damages only. The contract cannot be repudiated.

6   The correct answer is: By the parties themselves

Express terms are expressly agreed by the parties. The other options are examples of how terms are implied into contracts.

7   The correct answers are:

☑ The principle of freedom of contract states that parties may include in their contract any terms that they see fit.

☑ To be valid, a contract must be complete in its terms.

☐ Parties may not allow a third party to determine an essential term of the contract.

☐ Where a term is classified as a condition, the only remedy to an injured party if it is breached is to claim damages.

The principle of freedom of contracts states that parties are generally free to form a contract as they wish, but to be valid, a contract must be complete in its terms. Parties may include a term that allows a third party to determine an essential term. Where a condition is breached, the injured party may claim damages or treat the contract as discharged.

BPP
LEARNING
MEDIA

8   The correct answer is: By the courts

      The classification of an innominate term is determined by the courts where there is some dispute between the parties.

9   The correct answer is: The parties to a contract can expressly agree the terms of a contract.

      Express terms are agreed by the parties. The courts will imply terms for business efficacy, not fairness. Innominate terms can be implied by any method, or expressly agreed. Custom is a rare, and somewhat limited source of terms.

10   The correct answer is: By charter

      By charter – terms can only be incorporated by the express words of the parties, or, by implication via statute, trade custom or by the courts for business efficacy.

11   The correct answers are:

      ☐ A guarantee term
      ☐ A warranty term
      ☑ A condition term
      ☑ An innominate term.

      A breach of a condition will allow the injured party to repudiate, whilst an innominate term *may* give rise to this depending on how it is classified. A guarantee or warranty breach will result in an award of damages only.

12   The correct answer is: Where a contract breach leaves the injured party suffering a total loss of economic benefit they can sue for damages and repudiate the contract.

      Where a contract breach leaves the injured party suffering a total loss of economic benefit they can sue for damages and repudiate the contract – this describes a situation where an innominate term has been breached and is classified as a breach of a condition.

      An innominate term will render a contract void if breached – this is incorrect as a breach of such terms could be deemed a breach of a warranty, hence damages alone will be awarded.

      A condition of a contract results in an award of damages only if breached – incorrect, this leads to the right to repudiate also.

      A breach of a warranty leads to an award of damages designed to punish the breaching party – damages are designed to compensate the innocent party, not punish the breaching party.

13   The correct answer is: (i), (ii) and (iv) only

      Terms can be implied by statute, and by trade practice unless an express term in the contract overrides the trade practice.

      A court will imply terms in order to give the contract 'business efficacy' but will not imply a term to provide for events not anticipated at the time of agreement nor to override an express term.

14   The correct answer is: D Ltd can avoid the contract and recover damages.

      A condition is a major term in the contract. Breach of a major term entitles the injured party to avoid the contract and recover damages. If the term was a warranty, which is a minor term of a contract, then the injured party would only be entitled to sue for damages.

15   The correct answer is: Innominate term

Contractual terms are usually identified as being either conditions or warranties. Terms can be unclassified when the contract is formed and are known as innominate terms. They will be classed as either a condition or warranty once the effects of failure to fulfil it are known and assessed.

11 The employment relationship

1   The correct answer is: To provide references for the employee when the employee seeks other employment

There is no duty to provide references, although most employers do so. All the other options are duties of an employer.

2   The correct answer is: Both (i) and (ii)

Terms may be implied by a collective agreements and trade custom.

3   The correct answer is: An employer is obliged to provide an employee with a reference.

An employer is not required to provide a reference, but in practice most do. However, it must be accurate. All the other options are correct statements concerning employers.

4   The correct answer is: To provide an itemised payslip.

Providing an itemised payslip is a statutory duty. The other options are common law duties of the employer.

5   The correct answer is: Absence of error in work undertaken

The employee cannot be expected never to make mistakes. Only reasonable competence is required. Personal service and obedience to reasonable instructions are also implied duties of the employee.

6   The correct answer is: Dismissal on grounds of competence

Protection is provided by the Equality Act 2010 which protects against dismissal on the grounds of race, disability and sex. Lack of competence is a legitimate reason for dismissal.

7   The correct answer is: No. Deck Line Ltd was justified in its dismissal of Mick.

Although summary dismissal on liquidation is a breach of contract which can be treated as wrongful dismissal, Deck Line Ltd's liquidator is allowed to justify their action by reliance on evidence uncovered after the event (which is not the situation with unfair dismissal). Hence Mick's dishonesty justifies Deck Line Ltd's action.

8   The correct answer is: Compensation

Reinstatement and re-engagement are unlikely due to the breakdown in confidence between the parties. A punitive additional award would only be awarded if reinstatement or re-engagement had been awarded and the employer had ignored the order.

9   The correct answer is: (i), (ii), (iii) and (iv)

The auditor can be dismissed fairly because they are not permitted to practice as an auditor. The Finance Director can be dismissed fairly because they deceived their employer. The scientist can be dismissed fairly due to lack of competence and the warnings given to them. The solicitor can be dismissed fairly because redundancy is a fair reason for dismissal.

10 The correct answer is: Redundancy and unfair dismissal only

Dismissal occurs when a fixed term contract is not renewed, even though such an eventuality is implicit in the fact that the agreement has a fixed term. Nick is therefore entitled to claim for redundancy pay and/or compensation for unfair dismissal if he can prove the requisite facts. However, non-renewal cannot give rise to a claim for wrongful dismissal, which is only possible when there has been summary dismissal or dismissal with less than the required period of notice.

11 The correct answers are:

☐	Anne, who worked for 10 years and was given 9 weeks' notice.
☑	Barry, who worked for 1 week and was summarily dismissed.
☑	Catherine, who worked for 5 years and was given 2 months' notice.
☑	David, who has worked for 18 months and was given a week's notice.
☐	Emily, who worked for 6 months and was given 3 days' notice.

The statutory minimum notice period of 1 week for each year of employment is only relevant to people who have worked for 1 month or more, so Barry does not qualify. Emily should have been given a week's notice and Ann should have been given ten.

12 The correct answer is: Brian is entitled to 10 weeks' notice but Wye Ltd is entitled to only 1 week's notice.

Brian is entitled to 1 week for each year of his employment. The minimum period for an employee to give is 1 week.

13 The correct answer is: Damages under common law principles for breach of contract

Wrongful dismissal is a common law action against an employer for breach of contract and therefore damages are the usual remedy. The other remedies are available for unfair dismissal.

14 The correct answer is: (ii) only

It is possible for employees to bring claims of both wrongful and unfair dismissal. It does not follow that an unfair dismissal has to be a wrongful dismissal (for example a person can be unfairly dismissed but given the correct amount of notice).

15 The correct answer is: Constructive dismissal policy

Constructive dismissal is where an employee resigns under duress from the organisation. It is not part of the disciplinary process. Gross misconduct and summary dismissal would be covered.

12 Policies and practices

1   The correct answer is: Themselves and all others at the workplace

An employee is required to take reasonable care at work for the health and safety of themselves and others.

2   The correct answers are:

- [x] Bill has been indirectly discriminated against
- [ ] The company is legally required to employ a minimum number of disabled people
- [ ] Katie has been indirectly discriminated against
- [x] The manager's comments to Katie are discriminatory in nature

Bill has been indirectly discriminated against – the lack of equipment means that Bill is unable to perform the role because he is a wheelchair user.

The manager's comments to Katie are discriminatory in nature – the manager's comments are sexist in nature, and do not constitute legitimate or proportionate reasons for not employing women in the role.

There is no statutory requirement to employ a minimum number of any class of people, whilst Katie has been the victim of *direct* discrimination.

3   The correct answer is: Layering

Layering involves the transfer of monies to disguise their original source.

Placement is the disposal of the proceeds of crime into an apparently legitimate business property or activity.

Integration is the culmination of placement and layering, giving the money the appearance of being from a legitimate source.

Transposition is not a term related to money laundering.

4   The correct answer is: 14 years

There is a 14-year maximum prison term for laundering.

5   The correct answer is: Integration

Layering involves the transfer of monies to disguise their original source.

Placement is the disposal of the proceeds of crime into an apparently legitimate business property or activity.

Integration is the culmination of placement and layering, giving the money the appearance of being from a legitimate source.

Transposition is not a term related to money laundering.

6   The correct answer is: It is an offence for a corporation to fail to prevent bribery.

Bribery is a criminal offence. It can occur inside or outside the UK and corporations can be liable if they fail to prevent it. There are some exceptions to the law on bribery, for example relating to members of the armed forces or secret service who are on active duty.

7   The correct answers are:

- ☑ There is reasonable belief that it is substantially true
- ☐ There is reasonable belief that it is accurate
- ☐ There is reasonable belief that no one will suffer detriment from the disclosure
- ☑ There is reasonable belief that it is being made to the right person

These and good faith are the three elements of a protected disclosure.

8   The correct answer is: A payment made to an official to perform a routine function

Facilitation payments are a form of corruption. They are made to officials in return for them performing a routine function. For example a payment made to an official in return for them speeding up a travel visa application.

9   The correct answer is: A company that offers a client reasonable hospitality.

Reasonable hospitality is not bribery. Being bribed is an offence under the Act. Non-financial rewards are as much a bribe as the offer of cash. The Act extends around the globe and applies to all companies registered in the UK. It is also an offence for a corporation to fail to prevent an employee committing bribery.

10   The correct answers are:

- ☐ Tipping off
- ☐ Failure to prevent
- ☑ Laundering
- ☑ Failure to report

LT has assisted SP in laundering money through a criminal offence (tax evasion) and is also liable for failing to report SP's money laundering activities.

11   The correct answers are:

- ☐ The person did not expect to make a profit
- ☑ The person was exercising their function as a member of the intelligence service
- ☑ The person was exercising their function as a member of the armed forces on active service
- ☐ The person had reasonable grounds for their conduct

Only members of the armed forces or intelligence service that are properly exercising their function have a defence to bribery charges.

12   The correct answer is: All private individuals on whom only regulated data is held

Data protection legislation applies only to regulated data and is designed to protect the interests of private individuals only.

13   The correct answers are:

☑	Data must be processed lawfully
☐	Data can be processed for any purpose
☐	Data can be freely transferred between countries
☑	Data should be accurate
☑	Data should be relevant

Data transfers should be strictly controlled. Data can only be processed for lawful purposes.

14   The correct answer is: Individual managers failing to prevent bribery

There are four offences under the Bribery Act:

1.   Bribing another person (active bribery).

2.   Receiving a bribe (passive bribery).

3.   Bribing a foreign public official.

4.   Corporate failure to prevent bribery, where a company or partnership fails to put in place 'adequate procedures' to prevent offences being committed by an employee, agent or subsidiary.

15   The correct answer is: That the directors of the company are being paid excessively

A qualifying disclosure is any one of the following:

That a criminal offence has been committed, is being committed or is likely to be committed

That a person has failed, is failing or is likely to fail to comply with any legal obligation to which they are subject

That a miscarriage of justice has occurred, is occurring or is likely to occur

That the health and safety of an individual has been, is being or is likely to be endangered

That the environment has been, is being or is likely to be damaged

That information tending to show any matter falling within these categories has been, is being or is likely to be deliberately concealed

Clearly, pay of directors does not fall into any of these categories and therefore it is not a qualifying disclosure.

13 Legal personality

1   The correct answer is: Partnership

Partnership – the personal liability means that they are not running a private or public company. It cannot be a sole tradership as there are two business owners, hence it is a partnership.

2   The correct answer is: Disclosure and audit requirements

Disclosure and audit requirements – partnerships have little disclosure requirements and are exempt from audit.

The other options are advantages of running a company limited by shares.

3   The correct answer is: Where the directors are in breach of the regulations governing the giving of financial assistance for the purchase of the company's own shares

A court will 'lift the veil' if it is being used for the evasion of legal obligations, to recognise that a quasi-partnership relationship has broken down and where a group of companies has been operating as a single economic entity. Breach of financial assistance rules does not fall into these rules.

4   The correct answer is: Company can be sued in its own name

The other options are all back-to-front:

Company *can* enter into contracts in its own name

Company *can* own its own property

Management and ownership are *separated*.

5   The correct answers are:

✓	Fraudulent trading
	Company is being used to shield the owners from the debts of the business
✓	Company is being used to evade legal obligations
	When it is reasonable to do so

The correct answer options are: Fraudulent trading – possible per insolvency laws and company is being used to evade legal obligations - per the case of *Gilford Motor Co Ltd v Horne*.

A major advantage of the company form is the ability to use a company to shield the owners from the debts of the business eg confer limited liability.

The veil cannot be lifted merely because you feel it is reasonable to do so.

6   The correct answers are:

	The maximum number of members is limited
	The organisation's liability is limited
✓	The principle of perpetual succession applies
✓	The organisation can use floating charges when borrowing

In an incorporated organisation, the maximum number of members is unlimited and it is the member's liability that is limited. Unlike unincorporated organisations, they can use floating charges and the principle of perpetual succession applies.

7   The correct answer is: A company has full capacity to enter into contracts and can sue and be sued on them.

Due to the concept of separate legal personality, a company has capacity to enter into contracts and may sue and be sued on them.

8   The correct answers are:

✓	Perpetual succession
	Limited liability of the business organisation
	Shares may not be sold publicly
✓	Separate legal entity
✓	Limited liability of members.

A limited company is a legal entity separate from its members and has perpetual succession. Limited liability is that of the members not the company. Shares of public limited companies may be sold publicly. The question did not refer to a private company.

9   The correct answer is: (i) and (ii) only

Shareholders may incur additional personal liability if the corporate veil is set aside, depending on the circumstances.

10   The correct answers are:

✓	No requirement to file accounts
✓	All the profit accrues to the owner
	The business is liable for all business debts
✓	More control over the business than a company
	Easier to raise finance

Sole traders do not have to file accounts, all business profits accrue to the owner and the owner has more control than with a company because there are no shareholders. However, the owner rather than the business is liable for business debts and sole traders often find it difficult to raise finance because of the lack of security that limited liability provides.

11   The correct answer is: A private limited company

A private limited company – Gill will protect her personal assets via the veil of incorporation.

Each of the other options is an example of an unincorporated entity meaning there is no separation of Gills personal and business affairs, putting her house at risk.

12   The correct answer is: Ton Ltd

Adams v Cape Industries emphasises that companies within groups should generally be treated as separate legal entities. Therefore neither MBI plc nor the directors of MBI plc or Ton Ltd are liable.

13   The correct answer is: Yes, because the company has been formed as a device to mask Krystle's carrying on of the trade.

The facts are similar to *Gilford Motor Co v Horne*. The veil of incorporation will be ignored if the company was formed for an improper purpose (such as to allow the owner to compete where a covenant would otherwise prevent it).

14   The correct answer is: (i) and (ii) only

Failing to disclose the company's full name on company documents and fraudulent or wrongful trading are all valid reasons for lifting the veil of incorporation. Identifying the controlling mind of the company in corporate manslaughter cases is a common law (not statutory) reason to lift the veil. The corporate governance code is not legally binding so cannot be a reason to lift the veil.

15 The correct answers are:

☐ Increased disclosure
☐ Costs of administration
☑ Separate legal personality
☑ Transferability of ownership

The correct answers are: Separate legal personality – confers benefits such as limited liability and transferability of ownership – it is easier to sell shares than dispose of a partnership share.

Increased disclosure and costs of administration are *disadvantages* of running a company rather than a sole tradership or partnership.

14 Company formation and constitution

1 The correct answer is: Changing its register of members

The original members will be the formation agents, and when the company is purchased, the purchasers will want to become members themselves. None of the other changes are compulsory, though in practice all would generally occur.

2 The correct answer is: Negatively affects the company's reputation

Negatively affects the company's reputation – there is no reputational impact from purchasing a company off-the-shelf versus incorporating yourself. The other options are valid advantages of purchasing a company off-the-shelf as the owner does not need to wait for a certificate of incorporation to arrive.

3 The correct answers are:

☑ The articles of association set out the regulations governing the internal conduct of the company.

☐ The articles of association are registered with the Registrar of Companies after the Registrar has issued a certificate of incorporation.

☐ The articles of association are required for a public company, but not for a private company.

☑ The articles of association must state the company's name.

The articles set out the company's regulations. They are registered before incorporation, by both public and private companies, and contain the company's name.

4 The correct answer is: Public limited companies

Public limited companies must obtain a trading certificate before they can commence trading.

5   The correct answers are:

☐ Directors' remuneration

☑ Issue of shares

☑ Members' rights

☐ Appointment and dismissal of auditors

Directors' remuneration is decided by the Board of unlisted companies and the remuneration committee of listed companies.

The Articles regulate the appointment and dismissal of directors – not auditors.

6   The correct answer is: Articles of Association

Articles of Association – if you do not submit these the Registrar will adopt the relevant version on your behalf.

- To form a company you must submit:
- Name – ending in Ltd or Plc where appropriate
- Memorandum of Association – record of the intention of the subscribers to form a company
- Type – private or public company
- Registered office – address for receipt of legal notices
- Share capital – number and class of shares, plus their nominal value
- Directors – names and consent to act
- Shareholders – names of first shareholders
- Registration fee.

7   The correct answer is: (i) and (ii) only

A company's constitution binds the company and its members. Third parties are not bound.

8   The correct answer is: 6 years

Public companies must hold their accounting records for 6 years. Private companies must hold them for 3 years.

9   The correct answer is: Model articles of association describe how the company is to be managed and administered.

Model articles of association describe how the company is to be managed and administered. Companies can use any version of model articles that they like, and members are free to amend their contents. Model articles are prescribed by the Companies Act 2006 and updated through subsequent legislation rather than through the application of common law.

10   The correct answer is: Public limited companies must be audited, private limited companies are only required to have an audit if they meet certain financial criteria

It is compulsory for public limited companies to be audited. Private limited companies are only required to have an audit if they meet certain financial criteria.

11   The correct answer is: The date of the certificate of incorporation

The date of the certificate of incorporation – this is conclusive proof of the date that the company comes into existence, and thus can trade in its own name.

12   The correct answer is: They can be drafted by the company itself

They can be drafted by the company itself – though it is more common to adopt 'model' Articles prescribed by law. These can then be amended as the company sees fit.

They regulate the affairs of the partners – companies have Directors and Shareholders, not partners.

They regulate the payment of bonuses – they regulate payment of dividends not bonuses.

They cannot be altered – they can where sufficient numbers of shareholder agree to this.

13   The correct answer is: A company limited by guarantee

For companies limited by guarantee certain non-trading entities such as charities and educational establishments choose to adopt this company form as it allows them to drop the suffix 'Ltd' from some the company documents.

14   The correct answers are:

✓	Payment of dividends
	Payment of charitable donations
	Formation of a remuneration committee
✓	Appointment of directors

Payment of dividends and appointment of directors are included in the content of model articles of association. Payment of charitable donations and formation of a remuneration committee are not included.

15   The correct answer is: The content of model articles of association includes clauses relating to communication with members.

Communication with members is covered by model articles of association. Model articles differ depending on the type of company. They do not contain clauses on remuneration of employees or ethical treatment of suppliers.

Practice mock questions

1   **Which of the following describes how a framework-based approach to developing an ethical code differs from a rules-based approach?**

    ○   A framework-based approach sets out procedures to handle specific ethical dilemmas.
    ○   A framework-based approach requires members to follow the ethical code precisely.
    ○   A framework-based approach requires members to embody ethical principles.
    ○   A framework-based approach anticipates all potential ethical problems.

2   Tri Co is a large company which is undertaking a review of executive director remuneration.

    What does the UK Corporate Governance Code recommend for the structure of the remuneration committee?

    ○   They should mainly consist of executive directors.
    ○   They should mainly consist of non-executive directors.
    ○   They should only consist of non-executive directors.
    ○   There should be an equal mix of executive and non-executive directors.

3   **Which of the following statements in relation to misrepresentation are correct?**

    Select all that apply.

    ☐   To cause a misrepresentation, both parties to the contract must be aware of the misleading statement.

    ☐   To cause a misrepresentation, the public at large must be aware of the misleading statement.

    ☐   The misrepresentor will be liable if they know a misleading statement will be passed on to the other party.

    ☐   Silence by one party generally amounts to misrepresentation.

    ☐   Statements must be complete enough not to mislead.

4   You are visiting an old friend who happens to be an employee of a client that you are externally auditing. She has heard rumours that the company could be taken over by a competitor in the near future and is concerned about her job. You have heard the rumours as well and know that despite take-over talks having taken place, the interested buyer has decided not to proceed, and therefore your friend's job is safe. The two of you are alone at your friend's house when she asks you if you have any news about the take-over.

    Which of the following statements concerning your professional ethics is correct?

    ○   Because no one else will hear, you are permitted to tell her that the take-over is not going ahead.

    ○   There is a threat to confidentiality and therefore you must tell her that your professional ethics prevent you from commenting on the matter.

    ○   Your friend has asked you to comment on a rumour and to comment on it would be a breach of integrity, therefore you must tell her that your professional ethics prevent you from commenting on the matter.

    ○   Professional ethics do not extend to your personal life and therefore you can freely tell her that the take-over is not going ahead.

5   Lucy is a newly qualified member of CIMA and is keen to ensure that she follows the Fundamental Ethical Principles at all times. In her current role as an internal auditor, Lucy knows of the importance of demonstrating her independence.

Which of the following is an example of Lucy demonstrating her independence?

○   Double-checking her work
○   Avoiding situations that might cause an observer to doubt her objectivity
○   Questioning the work of others
○   Considering the needs of her colleagues at work

6   **Which TWO of the following are internal stakeholders in a business?**

☐   Employees
☐   Shareholders
☐   Directors
☐   Local community

7   Large Ltd has three shareholders, Alfie, Beatrice and Candice. Small Bank plc provides the organisation's other finance in the form of a secured loan and an overdraft. Spindle Ltd is a major supplier to the business, providing over 80% of the materials used the Large Ltd's products.

Which TWO of the following parties are contractually bound by Large Ltd's constitution?

☐   Alfie, Beatrice and Candice as shareholders
☐   Large Ltd
☐   Small Bank plc
☐   Spindle Ltd

8   Sally wants to purchase a car for her daughter. Her work colleague, Dan, tells her to phone his friend James who is trying to sell one. When Sally calls James, James tells her that he wants £1,000 for the car. Sally thinks this is a lot of money for the car and asks for a week to think about it and James said that he is happy to give her the time she needs. A couple of days later in the office, Sally mentions to Dan that she is still thinking about the car but Dan tells her that James sold it at the weekend. On hearing this, Sally immediately calls James to agree to pay £1,000 for the car.

Is there a valid contract and why?

○   Yes, because James agreed to keep the offer open.
○   No, because Sally's request to keep the offer open for a week was too vague to be binding.
○   No, because James' offer was revoked by Dan.
○   Yes, because James should have told Sally personally that he had sold the car.

9 Nisar is a qualified CIMA member. As a professional, he has a number of obligations that he needs to fulfil, such as following CIMA's Ethical Code, the law, his employment contract and contracts that his employer is bound by.

Which of the following is Nisar's secondary obligation to follow?

○ The law
○ CIMA's Ethical Code
○ His contract of employment
○ Contracts that his employer is bound by

10 **According to CIMA's publication "Fraud risk management: a guide to good practice", corruption is estimated to cost the global economy:**

○ $150 million
○ $1.5 billion
○ $150 billion
○ $1.5 trillion

11 Alice, Ben, Caroline and Deniz are all members of Holding Ltd's finance team. At a recent meeting, there was a discussion concerning what is required for certain types of contract to be valid.

Alice said, that to be valid, written contracts must be witnessed.

Ben said, that to be valid, oral contracts must be evidenced in writing.

Caroline said, that to be valid, deeds for the transfer of land must be in writing and signed.

Deniz said, that, to be valid, transfers of shares must be in writing.

Which TWO of the following members of the finance team are correct?

☐ Alice
☐ Ben
☐ Caroline
☐ Deniz

12 The OECD issued a number of general policies on corporate social responsibility.

Which of the following is NOT one of the OECD's general principles?

○ Be respectful of human rights.
○ Encourage local capacity.
○ Abstain from improper involvement in local political activities.
○ Prevent the formation of human capital.

13 **Which THREE of the following are characteristics of a traditional partnership?**

☐ Partnerships must have a minimum of two partners.
☐ Partnerships must be incorporated.
☐ Partnerships must perform some kind of business activity.
☐ Partnerships are based on the law of agency.
☐ Partners are only liable for contracts they personally signed.

14   The integrated reporting framework identifies six capitals to assess value creation.

Which THREE of the following are included in the six capitals?

☐ Manufactured

☐ Financial

☐ Academic

☐ Natural

☐ Cultural

---

15   When dealing with ethical dilemmas, accountants may apply the transparency, effect and fairness model.

Which of the following describes what an accountant would think about when considering transparency?

○ Identifying all parties that may be affected by the decision

○ Feeling comfortable about the decision and knowing the resulting actions are justifiable

○ Believing that a rational bystander would consider the outcomes reasonable on all concerned

○ Ensuring that the impact on key stakeholders is taken into account when making the decision

---

16   The Remuneration Committee of SCT Ltd is discussing changes to its remuneration policy for directors so that it complies with the UK Corporate Governance Code.

Which of the following aspects of the remuneration policy needs to be amended?

○ Directors should not be involved in setting their own pay

○ A significant amount of remuneration should be linked to corporate performance

○ Remuneration methods should promote the success of the business in the short-term

○ Levels of pay should motivate directors but not be excessive

---

17   **Which TWO of the following statements regarding contractual terms are correct?**

☐ Freedom of contract means that parties may include any contractual terms they like.

☐ Only contracts that are complete in their terms are valid.

☐ The law prevents third parties from setting essential contractual terms.

☐ Where a term is a condition, an injured party may only claim damages if it is breached.

---

18   Waseem is considering setting up a public limited company. In the past, he has bought a number of 'off-the-shelf' private limited companies, but this time wishes to register the company personally. However, he is unsure of the differences between setting up a private and a public limited company.

Which of the following documents is required only for public limited companies?

○ Memorandum of association

○ Trading certificate

○ Certificate of incorporation

○ Articles of association

19   Curtains plc is a listed company on the London Stock Market. Key members of the organisation are:

Arthur – the Chief Financial Officer (Finance Director)

Bayliss – the Company Secretary

Candice – the Chief Executive Officer (Managing Director)

Debbie – the Senior Non-Executive Director

According to the UK Corporate Governance Code, who may not act as the company's Chair?

- ○   Arthur
- ○   Bayliss
- ○   Candice
- ○   Debbie

---

20   **Which of the following are approaches to maximising the brand benefits of investment in Corporate Social Responsibility (CSR)?**

Select all that apply.

- ☐   Selective
- ☐   Stakeholder
- ☐   Integrated
- ☐   Environmental
- ☐   Invisible

---

21   **Which TWO of the following statements concerning ethical codes and the law are correct?**

- ☐   Criminal law is used to punish unethical behaviour.
- ☐   Student members of CIMA are expected to demonstrate the same professional standards as full members.
- ☐   Conflicts of interest are proof that unethical behaviour has occurred.
- ☐   Society's values are reflected in the law.

---

22   A team consists of the following four individuals:

Luke – who, when making decisions, looks for outcomes that benefit everyone

Margret – who, when making decisions, looks at the context of the decision and is prepared to be flexible and pragmatic

Nikita – who, when making decisions, looks at the fundamental correctness of an activity and is guided by laws and regulations

Oswald – who, when making decisions, looks after his own needs

Which member of the team is a pluralist?

- ○   Luke
- ○   Margret
- ○   Nikita
- ○   Oswald

---

23   Nigel is a trainee accountant working in practice. At a recent appraisal, Nigel's manager mentioned that he would benefit from following a programme of continued personal development, however, Nigel does not understand what benefits this would bring him.

Which of Nigel's skills and knowledge would benefit from a programme of continued personal development?

- ○   Communication skills
- ○   Accounting standards knowledge
- ○   Technical skills
- ○   Business awareness

---

24   Matthew and Debbie were married and owned their house jointly when they decided that they could no longer live together and separated. They agreed that Debbie would look after the children, but had to leave work to do so. Matthew agreed to pay Debbie maintenance of £3,000 per month on the condition that the mortgage was paid out of this, and that she transferred ownership of the house to him once the mortgage was repaid.

The agreement was put into writing and signed by both parties. Over the years, Matthew paid Debbie her allowance and Debbie continued to pay off the mortgage. However, once the mortgage was repaid, Debbie refused to sign over ownership of the house to Matthew.

Which of the following correctly describes the legal position between Matthew and Debbie?

- ○   Because Debbie did not provide any consideration for the agreement the contract is not valid. The issue of intention is not relevant.

- ○   Because Matthew and Debbie were married when the contract was signed, the courts will assume there was no intention to create legal relations. The contract is not valid. There is no issue in relation to consideration.

- ○   Because Matthew and Debbie were separated when the contract was formed, the courts will presume that legal relations were intended. The contract is valid. There is no issue in relation to consideration.

- ○   Because the consideration bought by each party to the contract was unequal the contract is not valid. The issue of intention is not relevant.

---

25   **Which THREE of the following are characteristics of the framework-based approach to ethical codes?**

- ☐   Discretionary
- ☐   Implicit
- ☐   Prevention
- ☐   Detection
- ☐   Mandatory

---

26 According to CIMA's ethical checklist, which THREE of the following is it important for CIMA members to do when resolving an ethical dilemma?

☐ Check all the facts

☐ Decide if the issue is legal in nature

☐ Identify affected parties

☐ Document their day to day feelings

☐ Seek advice from their families

27 The OECD has issued principles on business conduct.

Which of the following describes the nature of these principles?

○ Benchmarks to ensure that national codes comply with generally accepted best practice

○ Global, legally binding policies that all organisations must comply with

○ Regulations that are only legally binding on organisations whose governments have formally adopted them

○ Basic principles that organisations can choose to adopt or explain in the financial statements why they have not

28 As part of the audit planning process, audit engagement terms are usually agreed.

Which of the following is NOT party to the audit engagement terms?

○ The organisation's directors
○ The organisation's internal audit team
○ The organisation's shareholders
○ The external auditors

29 **Which THREE of the following are valid reasons for companies to establish corporate social responsibility (CSR) policies?**

☐ To meet legal obligations

☐ To meet customer expectations

☐ To improve staff retention

☐ To differentiate a brand name

☐ To improve the image of the business

30 **Which of the following are methods by which terms may be implied into contracts?**

Select all that apply.

☐ By statute

☐ By trade practice

☐ By courts, where circumstances occur which were not contemplated by the parties

☐ By courts, where the parties agreed the term but failed to express it because it was obvious

☐ By courts to override an express term

BPP LEARNING MEDIA

31 **Which of the following is an advantage of running a business as a company limited by shares, rather than as a limited liability partnership (LLP)?**

○ Company accounts are audited but the accounts of an LLP are not.

○ A company is a separate legal entity from its members, but an LLP is not.

○ A company may grant floating charges over its assets, but an LLP may not.

○ The personal property of a company's owners is protected from the insolvency of the company, but personal property of the partners in an LLP is not.

32 Four business partners are discussing setting up their business formally as a public limited company (plc). Each partner has a different view on plcs.

Annabel thinks that plcs must list their shares on a stock exchange.

Brian thinks that plcs must have at least one member.

Caz thinks that plcs must have at least two directors.

Derek thinks that plcs must have a company secretary.

Which of the business partners' view is wrong?

○ Annabel
○ Brian
○ Caz
○ Derek

33 An accountant amended their company's financial statements in violation of accounting standards because they did not think that the accounting standards were relevant to their company.

Which (if any) sets of values are conflicting?

○ Corporate and personal
○ Professional and personal
○ Professional and corporate
○ None

34 **Which of the following enables the Security and Exchange Commission to issue rules on corporate governance?**

○ The UK Corporate Governance Code
○ The Sarbanes-Oxley Act
○ The King Report III
○ The OECD Principles

35 Lynda is the Finance Director of a large airline. She recently made amendments to the company's accounting policy that has meant a number of accounting entries were made in violation of accounting standards.

Which type of error in the accounts did Lynda cause?

- ○ Error of commission
- ○ Error of principle
- ○ Error of omission
- ○ Error of authority

36 **Which school of ethics is advocated by CIMA?**

- ○ Virtue
- ○ Deontological
- ○ Utilitarianism
- ○ Consequentialist

37 **Which of the following are true statements concerning the UK's Corporate Governance Code?**

	True	False
All companies must state in their accounts whether they complied or did not comply with the Code.	☐	☐
The Code must be applied by all businesses that operate in the UK.	☐	☐
Directors will not face criminal liability if their company does not comply with the Code.	☐	☐
Directors may be sued by shareholders if their company does not comply with the Code.	☐	☐

38 **Which THREE of the following should an accountant consider when deciding how to resolve an ethical conflict with their employer?**

- ☐ Recent applications for promotion
- ☐ CIMA's ethical guidelines
- ☐ Internal grievance procedures
- ☐ The views of other CIMA members
- ☐ The consequences of potential resolutions

39 A company that has come under pressure over the sustainability of its manufacturing processes has decided to admit its culpability, but intends to keep fighting the negative press coverage it is receiving.

According to Carroll's social responsiveness model which approach is the company adopting?

- ○ Reaction
- ○ Defence
- ○ Accommodation
- ○ Proaction

40 **Which THREE of the following situations may create a conflict of interest?**

☐ Working part-time for two rival businesses

☐ Owning a small number of shares in a company that competes with your employer

☐ Being employed by a close relative

☐ Being offered a valuable gift by a friend who is also a business contact

☐ Receiving a performance bonus from your manager

41 **Indicate whether the following statements concerning the UK Corporate Governance Code are true or false.**

	True	False
The Code is a direct replacement for the law on directors' powers and duties that only applies to listed companies.	☐	☐
The Code provides alternative rules on directors' powers and duties that all companies can choose to follow instead of the law.	☐	☐
The Code provides rules on directors' powers and duties that companies may choose to follow in addition to the law.	☐	☐
The Code provides rules on directors' powers and duties that listed companies must follow or explain why they have not.	☐	☐

42 Janine has been asked to perform the following tests as part of an external audit for a client:

Test 1: Establish whether the receivables balance in the accounts is correct.

Test 2: Establish whether all creditor balances are included within the payables figure in the accounts.

Test 3: Establish the reason for an incorrect valuation in the inventory balance in the accounts.

Test 4: Establish where the figures for non-current asset additions have come from.

Which TWO of the following are 'substantive tests'?

☐ Test 1

☐ Test 2

☐ Test 3

☐ Test 4

43   Georgie is in dispute with her employer in regard to some terms that the employer says have been implied
      into her employment contract. The terms in dispute concern:

      •   Working hours: Her employer says these have been implied by legislation.

      •   Time off instead of being paid for overtime: Her employer says that this has been implied by a
           collective agreement between the trade union and the employer.

      •   Quality of work expected: Her employer says that this has been implied by what is customary in the
           industry.

      •   Acceptable use of the Internet: Her employer says that this has been implied by the employee
           rulebook.

      Which term is NOT implied into Georgie's employment contract?

      O   Working hours
      O   Time off instead of being paid for overtime
      O   Quality of work expected
      O   Acceptable use of the Internet

---

44   **Which of the following are statutory grounds for lifting the veil of incorporation?**

      (i)   Failure of a public company to obtain a trading certificate

      (ii)   The occurrence of fraudulent or wrongful trading

      (iii) Where a director of a liquidated company becomes a director of a new company with an identical or
             very similar name to the liquidated company

      (iv)   Where a listed company carries on business contrary to the UK Corporate Governance Code

      O   (i) and (iii) only
      O   (ii) and (iv) only
      O   (i), (ii) and (iii) only
      O   (i), (ii) and (iv) only

---

45   Ash is a very conscientious, newly qualified accountant. He always carefully double-checks all of work and
      calculations.

      By double-checking his work, Ash is protecting his:

      O   Objectivity
      O   Professional competence and due care
      O   Integrity
      O   Confidentiality

---

46   **Which TWO of the following were suggested by CIMA as improvements to global corporate governance
      codes?**

      ☐   Limiting the number of reports in the financial statements
      ☐   Linking the activities of the board to the key corporate events
      ☐   Demonstrating how the board works as a team
      ☐   Linking director remuneration to specific board activities

---

47   Certo Co has in the past outsourced the production of its products to whichever supplier charges the least cost per unit. This has caused a number of instances where the company's reputation has been damaged due to suppliers providing their workers with poor working conditions and paying them very low wages.

To prevent this from occurring in future, the company has decided to select suppliers on the basis of the quality of their product and on how their workers are treated, even if this means unit costs will rise.

Which TWO stakeholders may be in conflict as a consequence of this change in policy?

☐   Shareholders

☐   Employees

☐   Government

☐   Suppliers

☐   Competitors

---

48   **Which TWO of the following are bodies of the FRC's Conduct Committee?**

☐   Corporate Reporting Review Committee

☐   Case Management Committee

☐   Audit and Assurance Committee

☐   Corporate Reporting Committee

---

49   **Indicate whether the following statements describe elements of internal audit or external audit.**

	Internal audit	External audit
Responsible to the company's management	☐	☐
Opinion on truth and fairness	☐	☐
Follows professional standards and regulations	☐	☐
Testing is the main activity	☐	☐
Follows guidelines set by the company's management	☐	☐
No legal requirement to fulfil	☐	☐

---

50   A combination of impartiality, intellectual honesty and freedom from conflicts of interest.

Which of CIMA's fundamental principles does that statement describe?

○   Integrity

○   Professional competence and due care

○   Objectivity

○   Confidentiality

51   **Which THREE of the following are areas covered by the UK Corporate Governance Code?**

☐ Board leadership and company purpose

☐ Transparency and communication of information

☐ Division of responsibilities

☐ Corporate responsibility

☐ Remuneration

52   The International Integrated Reporting Council set out seven guiding principles that support the preparation of integrated corporate reports.

Which THREE of the following are included in the seven guiding principles?

☐ Consistency and transparency

☐ Reliability and completeness

☐ Professional presentation

☐ Conciseness

☐ Connectivity of information

53   **The FRC's Codes and Standards Committee consists of which of the following sub-bodies?**

Select all that apply.

☐ Audit and Assurance Council

☐ Corporate Reporting Council

☐ Corporate Reporting Review Council

☐ Case Management Council

☐ Actuarial Council

54   Unethical behaviour by individual accountants may have consequences for the whole accountancy profession.

Which THREE of the following are potential consequences to the accounting profession if accountants behave unethically?

☐ Professional bodies may lose their 'chartered' status

☐ Increased regulation of the profession by external organisations

☐ Increased employability of accountants

☐ Improved reputation of the profession

☐ Reduced public trust in the profession

55 **Which THREE of the following are included in IFAC's drivers for sustainable organisational success?**

☐ People and talent management

☐ Accounting excellence

☐ Effective and transparent communication

☐ Focus on the government and suppliers

☐ Effective leadership and strategy

56 **Which THREE of the following criteria must be met for audited financial statements to be considered true and fair?**

☐ Reflect the views of the board

☐ Free from error

☐ Factual

☐ Free from bias

☐ Reflect the commercial substance of the business' transactions

57 **Which of the following is NOT included on a statement of written particulars of employment?**

○ The name of the employer

○ The place of work

○ The intervals at which salary is paid

○ Entitlement to maternity and paternity pay

58 Dankwood Ltd has one director, Mel. Mel is also a member of the company and together with Smith they own all of the company's shares. Up until last year, the company employed Rowan as company secretary, but then Mel decided that the company does not need a company secretary and dismissed Rowan. Around the same time, Mel decided to advertise the sale of new company shares on the company's website, but no one took up the offer.

Which of the following company law rules has Dankwood Ltd breached?

○ Rules concerning offering shares to the public.

○ Rules concerning the number of members

○ Rules concerning the number of directors

○ Rules concerning a company secretary

59 **Which TWO of the following actions support an accountant in following the fundamental principle of professional competence and due care?**

☐ Spending enough time on a job to look into all matters in enough detail

☐ Not performing services that they cannot perform with reasonable knowledge, competence and diligence

☐ Only performing services that their employer has deemed them competent at

☐ Attending all training and technical update courses available to them even if not relevant to their job

60 **Which TWO of the following are criteria that should be met for a company to be exempt from an external audit?**

☐ Turnover less than £5.1m.

☐ Net assets less than £10.2m.

☐ Total assets less than £5.1m.

☐ Number of employees less than 50.

61 **Which THREE of the following are prerequisites for a fraud to occur?**

☐ Dishonesty

☐ Ability

☐ Motive

☐ Segregation

☐ Opportunity

62 **Which type of capital provides the infrastructure that enables organisations to deliver goods and services?**

○ Manufactured

○ Intellectual

○ Natural

○ Financial

63 The government of Eastland has decided to overhaul the country's approach to corporate governance and is considering a number of issues. The main decision is whether to use a principles or a rules-based approach to corporate governance.

Which of the following is NOT a matter that should affect the approach the government selects?

○ The state of the country's economy

○ The country's culture and history

○ The preference of company directors

○ The country's legal system

64 **Which of the following statements describes a rules-based approach to developing an ethical code rather than a framework-based approach?**

○ A rules-based approach sets out fundamental principles.

○ A rules-based approach attempts to anticipate every possible ethical dilemma.

○ A rules-based approach describes general guidelines for specific circumstances.

○ A rules-based approach expects members to comply with the spirit of the code.

65 The board of Rod plc (a large listed company) have just completed a review of the company's committee structure and have decided to make changes to the audit committee. However, the board needs to ensure that the formation of the committee complies with the UK Corporate Governance Code.

Which of the following suggestions for the structure of Rod Ltd's new audit committee complies with the UK Corporate Governance Code?

○ One executive director, one non-executive director and one accountant

○ Two executive directors and one non-executive director, all with recent and relevant financial experience

○ Three non-executive directors of which one has recent and relevant financial experience

○ Four executive directors, all with recent and relevant financial experience

66 **Which THREE of the following are aspects of the triple-bottom line?**

☐ Human capital
☐ Social justice
☐ Economic prosperity
☐ Cultural sustainability
☐ Environmental quality

67 Uptown Ltd collects data on its customers based on their use of its website and their buying patterns. The directors are concerned that its current data protection policy needs to be updated due to recent changes in data protection laws. To do this, the directors firstly want to determine which elements of the policy do comply with the legislation.

Which THREE of the following statements taken from the company's data protection policy comply with data protection legislation?

☐ Data must be processed fairly.
☐ Data can be processed for any purpose.
☐ Data must be destroyed after 10 years
☐ Data should be accurate.
☐ Data should be relevant.

68 Darren has recently been dismissed without notice and is considering claiming wrongful dismissal.

If Darren is successful in his claim, which of the following remedies might he be awarded?

○ Damages under common law principles for breach of contract.
○ Reinstatement.
○ Re-engagement.
○ Statutory compensation.

69 **Which TWO of the following statements concerning articles of association are correct?**

☐ The articles of association set out the regulations governing the internal conduct of the company.

☐ The articles of association are registered with the Registrar of Companies after the Registrar has issued a certificate of incorporation.

☐ The articles of association are required for a public company, but not for a private company.

☐ The articles of association must state the company's name.

70 Jan is an internal auditor who has recently completed a report for management. She has a large amount of calculations and analysis that support her findings.

Which of the following sections of her report should contain her calculations and analysis?

○ Executive summary
○ Appendix
○ Terms of reference
○ Conclusion and recommendations

71 CIMA and the Institute of Business Ethics jointly produced guidance to help organisations form an ethical policy (if they don't have one) or to help embed the policy into the organisation (if one exists).

Which of the following is NOT one of the aspects covered by the guidance?

○ Ensuring business behaviour reflects ethical values
○ Making ethical investments
○ Why produce a code of ethics?
○ Is a code enough?

72 **Which type of threat occurs when a professional accountant will promote a client's or employer's position to the point that their professional objectivity is compromised?**

○ Advocacy threat
○ Familiarity threat
○ Self-interest threat
○ Self-review threat

73 **Which of the following describes the impact of corporate governance on directors' powers and duties?**

	True	False
The Code recommends that company directors own shares in the company.	☐	☐
The Code recommends that companies establish an audit committee.	☐	☐
The Code recommends that companies establish a remuneration committee.	☐	☐
The Code recommends that both executive and non-executive directors attend the AGM.	☐	☐

74   **Which THREE of the following can help detect fraud?**

☐ Limitation controls
☐ Segregation of duties
☐ Reconciliations
☐ Control accounts
☐ Spot checks on employees

75   Ryan decided to make a number of disclosures about the directors of his company. He was aware that, as an employee under the Public Interest Disclosure Act (PIDA) 1998, he would be protected from dismissal and detriment if they are classified as qualifying disclosures.

Which THREE of following disclosures made by Ryan qualify under the Act?

☐ The directors were aware that criminal offences were being committed by the company, yet they did nothing to prevent them.

☐ The directors failed to ensure that the company met its legal obligations in connection with the disposal of toxic waste.

☐ The directors allowed the senior management team to claim excessive allowances.

☐ The directors have actively concealed unethical behaviour by its suppliers.

☐ The directors have allowed Ryan's health and safety to be endangered.

76   Zac has been asked to perform a number of activities as part of an external audit for a client.

Activity 1:   Examining material journal entries in the accounting system

Activity 2:   Reconciling the financial statements to the underlying accounting records

Activity 3:   Re-performing transactions listed in the accounting system

Activity 4:   Testing large volumes of predictable data by developing an expected balance, comparing to the actual data and reconciling any material differences

Which of the activities is an example of analytical review?

○ Activity 1
○ Activity 2
○ Activity 3
○ Activity 4

77   **Which THREE of the following statements concerning unfair dismissal are correct?**

☐   Employees can claim unfair dismissal regardless of their age.

☐   Employees can claim unfair dismissal after they have completed one year's employment.

☐   There is no upper limit on amount of compensation that can be paid to an unfairly dismissed employee.

☐   Unfair dismissal is a form of employment protection created by legislation.

☐   Employees who have taken part in official strike action are protected from unfair dismissal.

---

78   An accountant's work is questioned by a colleague and is found to contain material errors. The accountant acknowledges that they are responsible for these errors and agrees to correct them.

Which of the following professional qualities has the accountant demonstrated?

○   Independence
○   Accountability
○   Social responsibility
○   Scepticism

---

79   **Which TWO of the following statements regarding non-executive directors are incorrect?**

☐   Non-executive directors bring a wide range of experience and knowledge into the business.

☐   Non-executive directors will support the Chairman at directors' meetings.

☐   Non-executive directors have a wider perspective that may help the executive directors when they are involved in complex, operational issues.

☐   Non-executive directors eliminate the possibility of executive directors defrauding the company.

---

80   **Which THREE of the following aspects of operations are investigated as part of a value for money audit?**

☐   Efficiency
☐   Effectiveness
☐   Excellence
☐   Economy
☐   Equality

---

81   Aldo is an accountant who is responsible for producing the financial statements for XYC Co, a large manufacturing company, and has done so for many years. The company is an attractive takeover target because the last few year's accounts show high levels of profit and cash reserves. In recent weeks a number of potential buyers have come forward and the financial statements have come under a high level of scrutiny. Aldo was asked by XYC Co to attend meetings with the potential buyers to discuss the figures and he willingly did so. Aldo defended the figures in the accounts several times and described them as "100% accurate" and said "I've produced these accounts for many years and I am certain that they are correct."

After the meetings, Aldo looked again at his working papers and found an error in the accounts which has caused the profit figures to be overstated in each of the last three years.

BPP
LEARNING
MEDIA

Aldo's actions at the meetings has caused which of the following threats to his fundamental principles?

○ Familiarity threat
○ Self-interest threat
○ Intimidation threat
○ Advocacy threat

---

82 Audit evidence should be sufficient and appropriate.

Which TWO of the following are elements related to the appropriateness of audit evidence?

☐ Relevance
☐ Quantity
☐ Materiality
☐ Reliability

---

83 Adam, Belle, Colin, Dawn and Ed were all recently dismissed from Downsize plc. All employees of the company are only entitled to the minimum statutory notice period.

Adam worked for 1 year and was given 2 weeks' notice.

Belle worked for 12 years and was given 8 weeks' notice.

Colin worked for 5 years and was given 4 months' notice.

Dawn worked for 8 months and was given a day's notice.

Ed worked for 2 weeks and was given no notice.

Which THREE of the employees were given sufficient notice for dismissal?

☐ Adam
☐ Belle
☐ Colin
☐ Dawn
☐ Ed

---

84 **Which THREE of the following are included within the model articles of association?**

☐ Communication with shareholders
☐ Payment of dividends
☐ Payment of charitable donations
☐ Formation of an audit committee
☐ Removal of directors

85 **Which THREE of the following actions by an accountant demonstrates the professional quality of scepticism?**

☐ Keeping their mind free from distractions

☐ Seeking supporting evidence before accepting information is accurate

☐ Investigating why information was given to them

☐ Reviewing the work of a junior before accepting it as correct

☐ Being straightforward and honest at all times

Practice mock answers

1   The correct answer is: A framework-based approach requires members to embody ethical principles.

A framework-based approach, such as CIMA's, provides members with guiding principles that they are expected to follow.

The other options describe aspects of the rules-based approach to developing a code.

2   The correct answer is: They should only consist of non-executive directors.

The code states that remuneration committees should consist exclusively of non-executive directors.

3   The correct answers are:

- To cause a misrepresentation, both parties to the contract must be aware of the misleading statement.
- The misrepresentor will be liable if they know a misleading statement will be passed on to the other party.
- Statements must be complete enough not to mislead.

The statement may have been made to the public at large but there is no requirement for this (such as in an agreement between two individuals). Silence generally does not amount to misrepresentation because neither party is generally under any duty to disclose what they know (though exceptions to this rule exist - for example when applying for car insurance). The other options are all correct statements concerning misrepresentation.

4   The correct answer is: There is a threat to confidentiality and therefore you must tell her that your professional ethics prevent you from commenting on the matter.

Confidentiality means to safeguard the security of information unless there is a legal or professional right or duty to disclose. It also means not using information obtained in the course of work for personal advantage or for the benefit of others. Even though the friend will find out the good news about her job in due course, you should still respect confidentiality and not tell them. Professional ethics extend to your personal life.

There is no threat to integrity, this is related to be straightforward and honest in your business dealings.

5   The correct answer is: Avoiding situations that might cause an observer to doubt her objectivity.

Avoiding situations that might cause an observer to doubt her objectivity means that Lucy maintains her 'independence of appearance'. Double-checking work demonstrates integrity. Questioning work of others demonstrates professional scepticism. Considering the needs of others demonstrates respect.

6   The correct answers are:

- Employees
- Directors

Internal stakeholders such as employees, managers and directors are intimately connected to the organisation.

Shareholders are connected stakeholders - defined as either investing in, or having dealings with the firm. The local community and Government do not have direct links with the organisation and hence as external stakeholders.

7   The correct answers are:

- Alfie, Beatrice and Candice
- Large Ltd

Third parties (such as Small Bank plc and Spindle Ltd) are not contractually bound by a company's constitution.

8   The correct answer is: No, because James's offer was revoked by Dan.

James's offer has been revoked so there can be no contract. Revocation can be communicated by a reliable third party (as in *Dickinson v Dodds*). In this case, Dan can be seen as a reliable third party, because he has been involved in the process. Sally's request to keep the offer open is irrelevant since James is entitled to revoke his offer at any time.

9   The correct answer is: CIMA's Ethical Code.

The law always overrides professional and personal ethics as it is imposed to regulate society as a whole, whereas accounting's professional ethics only regulate the accounting industry. Therefore CIMA's Ethical Code is Nisar's secondary obligation. Employment and business contracts are entered into voluntarily and therefore an individual has a choice whether to comply with them or not.

10   The correct answer is: $1.5 trillion.

According to CIMA's publication "Fraud risk management: a guide to good practice", corruption is estimated to cost the global economy $1.5 trillion.

11   The correct answers are:

- Caroline
- Deniz

Most contracts can be completed verbally, however some 'specialty contracts' have certain requirements. These include written contracts which do not have to be witnessed but should be signed, and contracts for the sale of shares or transfer of land. There is no requirement for oral contracts to be evidenced in writing.

12   The correct answer is: Prevent the formation of human capital.

Prevent the formation of human capital.

The OECD's general principles of corporate social responsibility are:

- Be respectful of human rights.

- Encourage local capacity.

- Abstain from improper involvement in local political activities.

- Reject exemptions not contemplated in the regulatory framework related to environmental, health, safety, labour, taxation, financial incentives, or other issues.

- Encourage the formation of human capital.

13   The correct answers are:

- Partnerships must have a minimum of two partners.
- Partnerships must perform some kind of business activity.
- Partnerships are based on the law of agency.

By definition a partnership must consist of at least two partners and exist to perform some kind of business activity. The authority and liability of partners is based on agency law.

A traditional partnership is an unincorporated entity. All partners are jointly liable for the firm's debts.

14   The correct answers are:

- Manufactured
- Financial
- Natural

The six capitals are:

- Manufactured
- Financial
- Intellectual
- Natural
- Human
- Social and relationship

15   The correct answer is: Feeling comfortable about the decision and knowing the resulting actions are justifiable.

Feeling comfortable about the decision and knowing the resulting actions are justifiable shows transparency. Identifying and considering the impact on those affected by a decision shows that effect has been considered. Thinking about what a rational bystander would think about the outcomes shows fairness.

16   The correct answer is: Remuneration methods should promote the success of the business in the short-term.

According to the UK Corporate Governance Code, remuneration should promote the long-term success of the company. The other options all comply with the UK Corporate Governance Code.

17   The correct answers are:

- Freedom of contract means that parties may include any contractual terms they like.
- Only contracts that are complete in their terms are valid.

The principle of freedom of contracts states that parties are generally free to form a contract as they wish, but to be valid, a contract must be complete in its terms. Parties may include a term that allows a third party to determine an essential term. Where a condition is breached, the injured party may claim damages or treat the contract as discharged.

18   The correct answer is: Trading certificate.

Public companies must have a training certificate before they can trade or borrow. They also need a certificate of incorporation. Private companies just need a certificate of incorporation. Both private and public companies must have a memorandum and articles of association as part of the registration process.

19   The correct answer is: Candice.

The UK Corporate Governance Code recommends a clear division of power so that one person does not have unfettered powers of decision. Therefore the roles of chair and chief executive should not be performed by one person. The Code does not state that performing the other roles would prevent the person from also acting as Chair.

20   The correct answers are:

- Integrated
- Invisible
- Selective

The three approaches to maximising the brand benefits of investment in CSR are, selective, integrated and invisible. The other options are not known approaches.

21   The correct answers are:

- Student members of CIMA are expected to demonstrate the same professional standards as full members.

- Society's values are reflected in the law.

CIMA students are expected to demonstrate the same professional standards as full members and the law reflects societal values. Unethical behaviour is not always criminal behaviour. A conflict of interest describes a situation where an individual has competing professional or personal interests. It is virtually impossible for finance professionals to avoid conflicts entirely. It only becomes wrongdoing if the professional exploits the situation for his or her own benefit.

22   The correct answer is: Luke.

Pluralists look for outcomes that benefit everyone. Margret is a relativist. Nikita is an absolutist. Oswald is an egotist.

23   The correct answer is: Communication skills.

Personal development improves qualities such as communication skills which have to come from the individual. The other options describe technical knowledge and skills development.

24   The correct answer is: Because Matthew and Debbie were separated when the contract was formed, the courts will presume that legal relations were intended. The contract is valid. There is no issue in relation to consideration.

The courts will presume in the first instance that legal relations were not intended between man and wife, but the presumption is rebuttable. In this case, the facts that Matthew and Debbie are separated, the agreement is about property and is in writing would in all probability lead the court to presume legal relations were intended, as in *Merritt v Merritt*. Consideration does not have to be of equal value – Matthew agreed to pay Debbie £3,000 monthly and Debbie agreed to look after the children and pay the mortgage.

25   The correct answers are:

- Discretionary
- Implicit
- Prevention

The other characteristics of the framework-based approach include judgement, values driven, principles based, principles (values).

The other options are characteristics of the rules-based approach.

26   The correct answers are:

- Check all the facts
- Decide if the issue is legal in nature
- Identify affected parties

These options are all included in CIMA's ethical checklist.

There is no need to record personal feelings. Advice should not be sought from families as this may breach confidentiality.

27   The correct answer is: Benchmarks to ensure that national codes comply with generally accepted best practice.

The purpose behind the OECD principles is that they are to act as a benchmark to ensure that national codes all comply with generally accepted best practice. They are not directly binding on business organisations.

28   The correct answer is: The organisation's internal audit team.

The parties to an audit engagement letter are the auditors, managers/directors and the shareholders.

29   The correct answers are:

- To meet customer expectations
- To improve staff retention
- To differentiate a brand name

CSR involves going beyond legal obligations, not meeting them. Improving the organisation's image might result from CSR policies, but, morally, it should not be the reason to introduce them. Customers are increasingly expecting companies to be socially responsible, though, so this is a reason to adopt them. Socially responsible companies are able to attract and retain staff because they are pleasant places to work and being socially responsible helps differentiate a brand from others that are not so responsible.

30   The correct answers are:

- By statute
- By trade practice
- By courts, where the parties agreed the term but failed to express it because it was obvious

Terms can be implied by statute, and by trade practice unless an express term in the contract overrides the trade practice.

A court will imply terms in order to give the contract 'business efficacy' but will not imply a term to provide for events not anticipated at the time of agreement nor to override an express term.

31   The correct answer is: A company may grant floating charges over its assets, but an LLP may not.

A company may grant floating charges over its assets but an LLP may not.

The other options are incorrect – accounts of LLPs may be subject to audit and an LLP is a separate legal entity. Personal property of a company's shareholders and the partners of an LLP are both protected from the organisation's insolvency.

32   The correct answer is: Annabel.

A public company may offer some of its shares for sale to the public, but it is only compulsory if it is quoted on the stock exchange. All plcs must have at least one member, two directors and a company secretary.

33   The correct answer is: Professional and personal.

Their views are personal and accounting standards represent professional values.

Corporate values are those of the company itself.

34   The correct answer is: The Sarbanes–Oxley Act.

The Security and Exchange Commission is an American organisation and the Sarbanes–Oxley Act is American legislation regarding corporate governance rules.

35   The correct answer is: Error of principle.

Errors of principle occur during the recording a transaction in violation of accounting standards.

Errors of commission arise during the recording or posting of a transaction that has been recorded. Errors of omission are either partial or total omission from the books of prime entry. There is no such error of authority.

36   The correct answer is: Virtue.

In virtue ethics, justice, charity and generosity are dispositions to act in ways that benefit both the person possessing them, as well as society. This is the approach advocated by CIMA.

37   The correct answers are:

	True	False
All companies must state in their accounts whether they complied or did not comply with the Code.	☐	☑
The Code must be applied by all businesses that operate in the UK.	☐	☑
Directors will not face criminal liability if their company does not comply with the Code.	☑	☐
Directors may be sued by shareholders if their company does not comply with the Code.	☐	☑

Only listed companies must state in their accounts whether or not they complied with the Code. Non-compliance with the Code is not a criminal or civil offence and will not result in directors being sued by shareholders. The Code is only applicable to listed companies, although private limited companies may choose to apply it as best practice. There is no requirement for sole traders and partnerships to apply the Code.

38   The correct answer are:

- CIMA's ethical guidelines.
- Internal grievance procedures.
- The consequences of potential resolutions.

These are some of the matters that an accountant should consider when dealing with an ethical conflict.

The risk of missing out on promotion should not affect an accountant's decision on how to resolve an issue. By discussing their specific situation with others, an accountant will breach their duty of confidentiality and this should be avoided.

39   The correct answer is: Defence.

The four responses identified by Carroll include;

Reaction – denying responsibility
Defence – initially fighting responsibility, then do the least required to comply
Accommodation – accepting responsibility, and doing what is demanded of you
Proaction – volunteering to go beyond industry norms

40   The correct answers are:

- Working part-time for two rival businesses
- Being employed by a close relative
- Being offered a valuable gift by a friend who is also a business contact

Conflicts of interest are created when an accountant's objectivity is questioned. This may occur where they act for two rival business (would one be favoured over the other?), they are employed by a close relative (would they want to cause a rift with the relative?) and they are offered a gift (is it a bribe?).

Owning a small number of shares in a company that competes with your employer does not create a conflict of interest as you are not in a position to affect its results. The performance bonus would only cause a conflict if you were able to determine if you were eligible for reward.

41   The correct answers are:

	True	False
The Code is a direct replacement for the law on directors' powers and duties that only applies to listed companies.	☐	☑
The Code provides alternative rules on directors' powers and duties that all companies can choose to follow instead of the law.	☐	☑
The Code provides rules on directors' powers and duties that companies may choose to follow in addition to the law.	☑	☐
The Code provides rules on directors' powers and duties that listed companies must follow or explain why they have not.	☑	☐

The UK Corporate Governance Code adds additional powers and duties on top of existing legal duties, such as the need to engage constructively with shareholders and to manage risk responsibly. All companies may choose to follow the Code, but listed companies **must** comply with it or explain why they have not. Regardless of whether companies follow the Code, the law must always be followed as well.

42   The correct answers are:

- Test 1
- Test 2

Substantive tests 'substantiate' the figures in the accounts. They are used to discover whether figures are correct or complete, not why they are incorrect or incomplete, or how the figures 'got there'.

43   The correct answer is: Acceptable use of the Internet.

Terms may be implied into employment contracts by statute, common law, custom and collective agreements. Employee rulebooks may not be implied as contractual terms, however, disobeying them may amount to not following 'reasonable orders'.

44   The correct answer is: (i), (ii) and (iii) only.

Failing to obtain a trading certificate, fraudulent or wrongful trading and forming a company with a similar name to one which is insolvent are all valid reasons for lifting the veil of incorporation.

(iv) is incorrect as the UK Corporate Governance Code is not legally binding.

45   The correct answer is: Integrity.

Integrity is the important principle of honesty and requires accountants to be straightforward in all professional and business relationships. It also means not being party to the supply of false or misleading information.

Objectivity is a combination of impartiality, intellectual honesty and a freedom from conflicts of interest.

Professional competence and due care means accountants should refrain from performing any services that they cannot perform with reasonable care knowledge, competence, diligence and a full awareness of the important issues.

Confidentiality means to safeguard the security of information unless there is a legal or professional right or duty to disclose. It also means not using information obtained in the course of work for personal advantage or for the benefit of others.

46   The correct answers are:

- Linking the activities of the board to the key corporate events
- Demonstrating how the board works as a team.

One of CIMA's suggestions to improve global corporate governance codes is to demonstrate how the board works as a team. Other suggestions include:

- Including more specific reports in governance in the Chairman's statement.

- Linking the activities of the board to the key corporate events, using graphics if required to link actions to events.

- Communication and engagement with stakeholders explained via detailed reporting on how the investor relations were managed.

47   The correct answers are:

- Suppliers
- Shareholders

The policy will increase unit costs charged by suppliers and therefore reduce the amount of the company's profit available for distribution to shareholders in their dividend.

48   The correct answers are:

- Corporate Reporting Review Committee
- Case Management Committee

The FRC's Conduct Division monitors recognised supervisory bodies (such as CIMA), audit quality reviews, corporate reporting reviews, professional discipline and the oversight of the regulation of accountants and actuaries. It has three separate committees:

- Corporate Reporting Review Committee
- Audit Quality Review Committee
- Case Management Committee

49   The correct answers are:

	Internal audit	External audit
Responsible to the company's management.	✓	☐
Opinion on truth and fairness.	☐	✓
Follows professional standards and regulations.	☐	✓
Testing is the main activity.	☐	✓
Follows guidelines set by the company's management.	✓	☐
No legal requirement to fulfil.	✓	☐

External audit follows professional standards and regulations to test the company's financial statements in order to form an opinion about their truth and fairness as required by the Companies Act. It is ultimately responsible to the company's shareholders.

Internal audit will do anything the company's management requests and so may perform any activity (not just testing) and will follow any rules or guidelines required. It is ultimately responsible to the company's management. There is no legal requirement to conduct internal audit.

50   The correct answer is: Objectivity.

Objectivity is a combination of impartiality, intellectual honesty and a freedom from conflicts of interest.

Professional competence and due care means accountants should refrain from performing any services that they cannot perform with reasonable care knowledge, competence, diligence and a full awareness of the important issues.

Integrity is the important principle of honesty and requires accountants to be straightforward in all professional and business relationships. It also means not being party to the supply of false or misleading information.

Confidentiality means to safeguard the security of information unless there is a legal or professional right or duty to disclose. It also means not using information obtained in the course of work for personal advantage or for the benefit of others.

51   The correct answers are:

- Board leadership and company purpose
- Division of responsibilities
- Remuneration

The five areas covered by the UK Corporate Governance Code are:

- Board leadership and company purpose
- Division of responsibilities
- Composition, succession and evaluation
- Audit, risk and internal control
- Remuneration

52   The correct answers are:

- Reliability and completeness
- Conciseness
- Connectivity of information

The seven guiding principles are, strategic focus and future orientation, connectivity of information, stakeholder relationships, materiality, conciseness, reliability and completeness and consistency and comparability.

53   The correct answers are:

- Audit and Assurance Council
- Corporate Reporting Council
- Actuarial Council

The Codes and Standards Committee has three councils as sub-bodies; Audit and Assurance, Corporate Reporting and Actuarial.

The other options form sub-bodies of the Conduct Committee but are incorrectly stated as Councils when they are actually Committees.

54   The correct answers are:

- Professional bodies may lose their 'chartered' status
- Increased regulation of the profession by external organisations
- Reduced public trust in the profession

Professional bodies can lose their 'chartered' status if they are no longer seen to act in the public interest. The profession may be subject to external regulation or legal regulation by government if it cannot regulate itself adequately. The public will lose trust also.

Employability of accountants and the profession's reputation will be damaged if members behave unethically.

55   The correct answers are:

- People and talent management
- Effective and transparent communication
- Effective leadership and strategy

IFAC's drivers for sustainable organisational success are:

- Financial management
- Operational excellence
- Effective and transparent communication
- Customer and shareholder focus
- Effective leadership and strategy
- Integrated governance, risk and control
- People and talent management Innovation and adaptability

56   The correct answers are:

- Factual
- Free from bias
- Reflect the commercial substance of the business' transactions

An audit provides assurance that the financial statements are free from material misstatement not error. They should show the facts, not the views of the board which may be biased. Truth and fairness is based on the principles that the financial statements are factual, free from bias and reflect the commercial substance of the business' transactions.

57   The correct answer is: Entitlement to maternity and paternity pay.

Entitlement to maternity and paternity pay is not required as these are statutory rights.

The statement should identify the following:

- The names of employer and employee
- The date on which employment began
- Whether any service with a previous employer forms part of the employee's continuous period of employment Pay-scale or rate and intervals at which paid
- Hours and place of work (including any specified 'normal working hours')
- Any holiday and holiday pay entitlement (the statutory minimum is 28 days which may include public holidays)
- Sick leave and sick pay entitlement
- Pensions and pension schemes
- Length of notice of termination to be given by either side
- The title of the job which the employee is employed to do (or a brief job description)

58   The correct answers are: Rules concerning offering shares to the public.

A private company may be formed and operate with only one member and one director. A company secretary is not required, though if you are the sole director of a private company you cannot also perform the functions of a Company Secretary. Shares cannot be offered to the public either by the company itself or by the shareholders.

59   The correct answers are:

- Spending enough time on a job to look into all matters in enough detail.
- Not performing services that they cannot perform with reasonable knowledge, competence and diligence.

Professional competence and due care means accountants should refrain from performing any services that they cannot perform with reasonable care knowledge, competence, diligence and a full awareness of the important issues. They should spend sufficient time to look into all matter sufficiently.

Accountants should not accept work from their employers if they do not believe themselves competent. Accountants are only required to stay technically up-to-date in areas relevant to their current role.

60   The correct answers are:

- Total assets less than £5.1m.
- Number of employees less than 50.

The criteria for exemption from audit are:

- Turnover less than £10.2m.
- Total assets less than £5.1m.
- Number of employees less than 50.

61   The correct answers are:

- Motive
- Opportunity
- Dishonesty

The three elements which must be place for fraud to occur are dishonesty, motive and opportunity.

62   The correct answer is: Manufactured.

Manufactured capital is the infrastructure available to help the organisation deliver goods and services. Natural capital consists of available environmental resources such as oil, gas and coal. Financial capital is the pool of investment funds available to a company. Intellectual capital includes intangible assets such as patents and licenses.

63   The correct answer is: The preference of company directors.

The preference of company directors should not be a consideration because it may be biased and be incompatible with issues such as the country's legal system, economy and culture and history which may actually affect how the corporate governance system works in practice (eg the legal system will impact on the ability of courts to interfere with how companies are run).

64   The correct answer is: A rules-based approach attempts to anticipate every possible ethical dilemma.

A rules-based approach attempts to set rules that can be applied in every possible circumstance. The other options describe the framework-based approach to developing a code.

65   The correct answer is: Three non-executive directors of which one has recent and relevant financial experience.

For a large company, an audit committee should consist entirely of non-executive directors. There should be at least three, and at least one of those should have recent and relevant financial experience.

66   The correct answers are:

- Social justice
- Economic prosperity
- Environmental quality

The three aspects to the triple-bottom line are economic prosperity, social justice and environmental quality.

67   The correct answers are:

- Data must be processed fairly.
- Data should be accurate.
- Data should be relevant.

Data can only be kept for as long as it is needed and therefore may need to be destroyed before 10 years is up. Data can only be processed for lawful purposes.

68   The correct answer is: Damages under common law principles for breach of contract.

Damages under common law principles for breach of contract.

Wrongful dismissal is a common law action against an employer for breach of contract and therefore damages are the usual remedy. The other remedies are only available for unfair dismissal.

69   The correct answers are:

- The articles of association set out the regulations governing the internal conduct of the company.
- The articles of association must state the company's name.

The articles set out the company's internal regulations, not its vision or mission. They are registered before incorporation, by both public and private companies, and contain the company's name.

70   The correct answer is: Appendix.

Terms of reference define the scope of the investigation. The executive summary is a high level summary of the report, the appendix contains supporting analysis and the conclusion and recommendations contains the findings of the report and sets out what should be done next.

71   The correct answer is: Making ethical investments.

Making ethical investments is not covered by the guidance. The other aspects are.

72   The correct answer is: Advocacy threat.

An advocacy threat is the risk that an accountant promotes a client's or employer's position to the point that their objectivity is compromised.

A self-interest threat is the risk that a financial or other interest may influence the accountant's judgement or behaviour. It is also known as a 'conflict of interest' threat.

A familiarity threat is the risk that due to a long or close relationship with a client or employer, an accountant will be too sympathetic to their interests or too ready to accept their work.

A self-review threat is the risk that an accountant may not appropriately re-evaluate their (or a colleague's) previous work (including judgements made or services performed) when relying on the work while performing a current service.

73   The correct answer is:

	True	False
The Code recommends that company directors own shares in the company	☐	☑
The Code recommends that companies establish an audit committee	☑	☐
The Code recommends that companies establish a remuneration committee	☑	☐
The Code recommends that both executive and non-executive directors attend the AGM	☑	☐

While share ownership and executive options are commonplace they are neither recommended nor mandated. The code suggests that companies should have audit and remuneration committees and that all board members should attend the AGM.

74   The correct answers are:

- Reconciliations
- Control accounts
- Spot checks on employees

Segregation of duties and limitation controls help prevent (not detect) fraud. The other options detect fraud because they are checks on whether the system or processes are being followed correctly. The fact these controls are in place will also help deter, though not eliminate, fraud from occurring.

75   The correct answers are:

- The directors were aware that criminal offences were being committed by the company, yet they did nothing to prevent them.

- The directors failed to ensure that the company met its legal obligations in connection with the disposal of toxic waste.

- The directors have allowed his health and safety to be endangered.

A qualifying disclosure is any one of the following:

- That a criminal offence has been committed, is being committed or is likely to be committed.

- That a person has failed, is failing or is likely to fail to comply with any legal obligation to which they are subject.

- That a miscarriage of justice has occurred, is occurring or is likely to occur.

- That the health and safety of an individual has been, is being or is likely to be endangered.

- That the environment has been, is being or is likely to be damaged.

- That information tending to show any matter falling within these categories has been, is being or is likely to be deliberately concealed.

76 The correct answer is: Activity 4.

Testing large volumes of predictable data by developing an expected balance, comparing to the actual data and reconciling any material differences.

Re-performing transactions is an example of a test of control. Examining material journal entries and reconciling financial statements to underlying accounting records are examples of substantive tests. Testing large volumes of predictable data by developing an expected balance, comparing to the actual data and reconciling any material differences describes analytical review.

77 The correct answers are:

- Employees can claim unfair dismissal regardless of their age.
- Unfair dismissal is a form of employment protection created by legislation.
- Employees who have taken part in official strike action are protected from unfair dismissal.

Unfair dismissal was created by the Employment Rights Act 1996. Employees must have been employed for at least 2 years before claiming unfair dismissal, but can be of any age. Compensation is capped by legislation, which is reviewed annually. Employees who have taken part in official strike action cannot be dismissed in connection with the strike.

78 The correct answer is: Accountability.

Accountants are responsible for their own work. Acknowledging this demonstrates accountability.

Independence means avoiding conflicts of interest. Social responsibility means acting in the public interest. Scepticism means questioning information given to you and making your own mind up about it.

79 The correct answers are:

- Non-executive directors will support the Chairman at directors' meetings.
- Non-executive directors eliminate the possibility of executive directors defrauding the company.

Non-executive directors bring experience, knowledge and a wider perspective into the company. They bring a strong, independent element on the Board, and are not there to act as 'henchmen' to enable the Chairman to get their own way. Although the presence of non-executive directors may help deter fraud, they will never eliminate it.

80 The correct answers are:

- Economy
- Efficiency
- Effectiveness

A value for money audit is an audit of how to improve the economy, efficiency and effectiveness of operations.

81   The correct answer is: Advocacy threat.

Advocacy threats are created when an accountant promotes their client's or employer's position to the extent that their objectivity is compromised. Aldo's actions in declaring his work as '100% accurate' have made it very difficult for him to go back and admit the error.

Familiarity threats result from being too close to the work so you cannot be objective. This may have caused the error in the first place but it is not the threat caused by Aldo's actions in the meetings. Self-interest is the threat that a financial/other interest will inappropriately influence the accountant's judgment or behaviour - there is no suggestion here that Aldo is motivated by self-gain arising from his mistakes.

Intimidation threats are created by third parties putting pressure on the accountant, there is no such pressure here.

82   The correct answer is:

- Relevance
- Reliability

Relevance and reliability are related to the appropriateness of evidence. Quantity relates to the sufficiency of audit evidence. Materiality is not related to sufficiency or appropriateness.

83   The correct answers are:

- Adam
- Colin
- Ed

The statutory minimum notice period is 1 week for each year of employment and is only relevant to people who have worked for 1 month or more, so Ed does not qualify. Belle should have been given 12 weeks' notice and Dawn should have been given a week.

84   The correct answers are:

- Payment of dividends.
- Removal of directors.
- Communication with shareholders

Payment of dividends, removal of directors and communication with shareholders are included in the content of model articles of association. Payment of charitable donations and formation of an audit committee are not included.

85   The correct answers are:

- Seeking supporting evidence before accepting information is accurate.
- Investigating why information was given to them.
- Reviewing the work of a junior before accepting it as correct.

The correct options demonstrate questioning and non-acceptance that work is correct on face value. Being straightforward and honest demonstrates integrity. Keeping your mind free from distractions demonstrates objectivity.

BPP
LEARNING
MEDIA

Tell us what you think

Got comments or feedback on this book? Let us know.
Use your QA code reader:

Or, visit:

https://www.smartsurvey.co.uk/s/VN5OFD/